WHY ISRAEL?

Understanding Israel, the Church, and the Nations in the Last Days

WHY ISRAEL?

Understanding Israel, the Church,
and the Nations in the Last Days

WILLEM J.J. GLASHOUWER

DESTINY IMAGE EUROPE™ srl
Via Maiella, 1
66020 San Giovanni Teatino (Ch) - Italy

"Changing the world, one book at a time."

This book and all other Destiny Image Europe™ books are available at Christian bookstores and distributors worldwide.

To order products, or for any other correspondence, please contact:

DESTINY IMAGE EUROPE™ srl
Via Acquacorrente, 6
65123 - Pescara - Italy
Tel. +39 085 4716623 - Fax: +39 085 9431270
E-mail: info@eurodestinyimage.com

Or reach us on the Internet: **www.eurodestinyimage.com**

ISBN-13: 978-88-89127-52-0

For Worldwide Distribution, Printed in the U.S.A.

1 2 3 4 5 6 7 8/10 09 08 07

Dedication

To Karel van Oordt, the founding father of Christians for Israel, who over the years has inspired me and many others to understand the mystery of Israel, and has taught us to bless the Jewish people and the nation of Israel.

Contents

Foreword

It is a great pleasure for me to write the Foreword to the English edition of Willem Glashouwer's *Why Israel?* I have no doubt in my mind that the Lord miraculously spared Willem in the massive brain operation that he endured, a story he tells in the fifth chapter of this book. At the least he could have been left a mute, or at the best greatly impaired. Instead, he is an indefatigable and untiring servant of the Messiah, the Lord Jesus, traveling the world and preaching everywhere. Indeed, considering this operation, he is one of the most clear, concise, and anointed preachers of the Word of God in our generation.

Why Israel? has all to do with another and even greater miracle that the Lord has worked in our modern times, the re-creation of the State of Israel within her original homeland. Both the author and his subject are modern miracles. The title is both arresting and apposite! The question asked is simple but to the point. More than half of the world questions the right of Israel to her statehood and even more to the land in which it happened. It was once described in evangelical circles as the "Promised Land"; today it is a term rarely used.

The focal point of all this controversy and confusion is modern Israel. At present, it does not seem that it will abate but rather grow in its intensity. With the growth of fanatical Islamic fundamentalism, the rise of Iran as a new regional superpower, the repeated declaration of her President Ahmadinijead to "wipe Israel off the face of the world map," the funding, arming, and training by Iran of Syria, Hezbollah in the Lebanon, and of Hamas in the Gaza Strip, the outlook for the Middle East and indeed for the world is increasingly grim. It is no wonder that many of us with long memories feel that we are witnessing a rerun of the years leading to the Nazi Holocaust. This growing furor amongst the nations concerning Israel will not dissipate but become more hate filled and determined. If they cannot annihilate Israel, they will attempt at least to undo the Balfour Declaration, reducing Israel to size and rendering her indefensible. The two-state solution is all part of this satanic attempt. From the beginning, satan has hated the Jewish people as he also hates the true Church and knows that his time is short.

If the presence of Israel on the world stage is considered a coincidence, the product of human ingenuity and intelligence, it must be the most remarkable and indeed incredible coincidence in history. No other nation has twice been exiled from its national territory, suffered the destruction of its national institutions and infrastructure and been exiled, and then returned to the exact same location. The first time it was for fifty years, a thousand miles east, and the second time it was for at least one thousand eight hundred years and into every part of this earth. No other nation has lost its mother tongue, Hebrew, and had it restored as the mother tongue of at least three and a half million people. Every part of modern Israel is a unique miracle of resurrection and re-creation, from the cities and towns that have been ruined for thousands of years and now rebuilt, from eroded soil mountains and hills that are now covered with forest, from swamplands that are now fields, from infertility to fertility, and so I could go on. Is all of this a coincidence, the result of human ingenuity and intelligence?

One must never forget that Israel rose from the ashes of the Holocaust. When she was most desolate, most brokenhearted and at her weakest point,

God worked the miracle. It is simpler to believe that it is the hand of God in history. The basic fact that the Word of God throughout the Old Testament, and at crucial points in the New Testament, declares this truth, should be enough for those born of the Spirit of God. Israel's presence is miraculous and in the years ahead will be seen to be ever more so.

There is a phrase in the sixth chapter of this book that Willem has used, in his own inimitable way, which I believe goes to the root of the matter: "For Israel is a designated sign of God in the world." Her resurrection, her re-creation as a state, her survival through the sixty years of her modern history with its eight wars, are evidence of something God has constituted. The Lord is speaking to the nations ever more clearly and loudly through Israel, even while she is still in her unbelief and disobedience. The apostle Paul prophetically declares, "As touching the election, they [Israel] are beloved for the fathers' sakes. For the gifts and calling of God are without repentance [irrevocable]" (Romans 11:28b-29 KJV). Irrevocable is irrevocable, just as election is election! No matter how much the forces of darkness come against Israel, they will fail and she will triumph.

Thus Israel, misrepresented, hated, and increasingly isolated, will be divinely prepared for the miracle of her salvation. There is a phrase found in the story of Jacob that is pregnant with prophetic meaning for the modern state of Israel—"And Jacob was left alone" (Gen. 32:24 KJV). Only then did the heavenly visitor, surely the Messiah Himself, appear and wrestle with him until he became God's Israel. In some marvelous manner, the Deliver will come out of Zion, and turn away ungodliness from Jacob (see Gen. 32:24-30; Rom. 11:25-27). The same fathomless love and grace of God that has saved every Gentile sinner who has put their trust in Him will save Israel.

Willem Glashouwer, with his fine biblical scholarship and his shrewd discernment, has rendered us a great and invaluable service in writing this book. May the Lord bless it and use it for the enlightenment of many!

Lambert Lance
International Author and Bible Teacher
Jerusalem, Israel

Introduction

During the years as chairman of Christians for Israel (Holland), and now as president of Christians for Israel International (Website: www.c4israel.org), I often speak, preach, and teach from the Bible about Israel. People sometimes ask me, "Why are you so involved with Israel and the Jewish people? Is it a kind of hobby for you, like collecting stamps or playing golf? Why Israel? What's so special about Israel?"

My answer is always, "Well, I hope that what I feel about Israel is similar to what God feels about them. God loves Israel. Jesus loves Israel. The Bible says so. And because I love Jesus, and I know that He loves me, I can't help loving the people He loves."

My involvement with Israel began when someone once said to me, "You know, there are many Christians who love 'dead Jews.'" I replied, "I beg your pardon…'dead Jews'?" "Yes," he exclaimed, "the Jews of the past—Moses, Joshua, Isaiah, Jeremiah, David, Paul, Peter, John, and all the others. The Jews of the Bible—Jews who are long gone." He proceeded to say, "And then there are Christians who love Jews who are not yet born—the Jewish generation who will live in the prophetic future when Israel will be the center of the earth, and Jerusalem will be the city from which peace will flow out and fill the earth.

"But who will stand with the Jewish people today? Who will love them in the name of Jesus? Who will remain at their side while the world strives against them? Who will plead with the Church to repent of her terrible past? Who will start reading the Scriptures again to discover what the real relationship is between Israel and the Church? What about the Church's Jewish roots? What about our prophetic future together? While the Church and Israel might have very different views about who the Jew, Jesus, really is, the fact is this difference doesn't mean much to the powers of darkness. Those powers hate both peoples of God—both who believe in the same God; those powers will persecute Bible-believing Christians just as much as they will the Jews and Israel. History makes this quite clear."

What he said made a great impact and encouraged me to start thinking and asking questions, such as, "What has God to do with Israel...even today? Even after the vast majority of the Jewish people have rejected Jesus as their Messiah and as the Son of God?" These questions drove me to reread the Scriptures, both the Old and New Testament—God's totally trustworthy Word that He has revealed to the Jewish people.

Searching the Scriptures, it slowly dawned upon me that God has established everlasting covenant relationships with Israel, and He has never abolished these covenant promises. In that sense, Israel has not been replaced by the Church. All the promises He has made to Israel He will fulfill for Israel. In the same way, He will fulfill all the promises He has made to the Church.

May the Lord bless your discovery tour through the Scriptures, guided by the following pages, so that you become more prepared for the glorious coming of the Lord!

Rev. Willem J.J. Glashouwer

CHAPTER ONE

Israel: God's Firstborn

GOD LOVES AND DISCIPLINES HIS FIRSTBORN

Upon being encouraged to think about what God has to do with Israel today, I began to reread and study the Scriptures, both the Old and New Testament. The first thing I discovered was that while Jesus is God's only begotten Son (see John 1:14), Israel is His firstborn son. When the children of Israel were oppressed slaves in Egypt and Pharaoh refused to let them go while systematically increasing their hardship in order to reduce their numbers, Moses and his brother Aaron sent Pharaoh this message: *"This is what the Lord says: Israel is My firstborn son, and I told you, 'Let My son go, so he may worship Me.' But you refused to let him go; so I will kill your firstborn son"* (Exod. 4:22b-23). And that was what happened in the tenth plague that struck Egypt: *"At midnight the Lord struck down all the firstborn in Egypt, from the firstborn of Pharaoh, who sat on the throne, to the firstborn of the prisoner, who was in the dungeon, and the firstborn of all the livestock as well"* (Exod. 12:29). Refusing to let God's firstborn son go did indeed cost them their firstborn sons, as God had warned.

For God loves the Jewish people as a father loves his child. The prophet Hosea records God's emotions in the lament that begins: *"When Israel was a child, I loved him, and out of Egypt I called My son"* (Hos. 11:1). God speaks as a father about His often disobedient and delinquent son, with all the conflicting emotions, from tender love to great anger, that a father can feel. Anyone with children of their own will understand these emotions. You love your children and will do anything for them, but their behavior can sometimes make your blood boil! And then you'll speak harsh or sharp words, or words of warning, because you see that ultimately things will go terribly wrong if they continue to behave in that way. Out of concern and out of love, you speak words of correction, and possibly even take disciplinary action. As an old Dutch proverb says: If they won't hear, they must feel!

One can hear the frustrated anger of the Father when He says, *"But the more I called Israel, the further they went from Me. They sacrificed to the Baals* [idols] *and they burned incense to images"* (Hos. 11:2). "I did everything possible for My son," God says. *"It was I who taught Ephraim* [a term of endearment for Israel] *to walk* [just as a father teaches his children their first baby steps] *taking them by the arms* [as a father takes toddlers who have fallen into his arms to comfort them]; *but they did not realize* [or recognize] *it was I who healed them"* (Hos. 11:3). In other words, God says, "I put plasters on their scratches and bruises, as an earthly father would do. But were they grateful? Absolutely not!"

"I led them with cords of human kindness, with ties of love" (Hos. 11:4a). Just like earthly parents, God used every means to express love to bring His people back to Himself. *"I lifted the yoke from their neck and bent down to feed them"* (Hos. 11:4b). Like harnessed oxen pulling a plow, the people had sighed under the slavery of Egypt, driven along prescribed paths. But the Lord broke the yoke that harnessed them and freed His people from the slave drivers. He guided them across the Red Sea and into the desert (see Exod. 13–14), and there He provided for their needs with manna from Heaven and water from the rock. He led them from resting place to resting place, from oasis to oasis. Yes, He even provided meat in the form of quails (see Exod. 16–17:7). *"I...bent down to feed them"* (Hos. 11:4b).

And then we hear the anger in His voice. *"Will they not return to Egypt* [back to slavery! That's what they deserve, with their ingratitude!] *and will not Assyria rule over them?"* (Hos. 11:5a). What Assyria did to its prisoners of war is too cruel to describe on paper, although it is chiselled in the rocks where the Assyrian kings immortalized their horrendous deeds. And it is to Assyria that the ten tribes of Israel were finally led into captivity (see 2 Kings 17:23) *"…because they refuse to repent? Swords will flash in their cities, will destroy the bars of their gates and put an end to their plans"* (Hos. 11:5b-6). In other words, God says, "They can only blame themselves and their own behavior." *"My people are determined to turn from Me"* (Hos. 11:7a).

Hosea, the prophet, adds his personal opinion: *"Even if they call to the Most High, He will by no means exalt them"* (Hos. 11:7b).

THE APPLE OF GOD'S EYE

But once again, the love in the heart of the Father breaks out. You can't look on with dry eyes, can you? No matter what your child, your son, has done, isn't he still your son? Of course, he is. Therefore, God says, *"How can I give you up, Ephraim? How can I hand you over, Israel? How can I treat you like Admah? How can I make you like Zeboiim?"* (Hos. 11:8a). Admah and Zeboiim were cities in the rift of the Dead Sea that were destroyed by fire from Heaven along with Sodom and Gomorrah, because of God's wrath (see Deut. 29:23). "Can I do this to My own firstborn son?" God asks. Discipline him, yes! But reject him? Never! Will he not always remain your son, your firstborn, your own child? *"My heart is changed within Me; all My compassion is aroused. I will not carry out My fierce anger, nor will I turn and devastate Ephraim. For I am God, and not man—the Holy One among you…"* (Hos. 11:8b-9).

People can act with great cruelty, and the actions of the nations who came against God's firstborn son, Israel, were just that—cruel. God says by the mouth of the prophet Zechariah, *"I am very angry with the nations that feel secure. I was only a little angry, but they added to the calamity"* (Zech. 1:15). God says, "I know how to find these nations! I will judge those nations!" The great judgment of God on the nations will eventually come, in accordance with what they have done to Israel, because Israel is the apple of God's eye (see Zech. 2:8-9).

Your eye is the most sensitive part of your body. Merely flicking a finger near your eye is enough to make you recoil. When directors of horror movies really want to shock their audiences, they know what to do—they mutilate eyes, sometimes even slicing them with razors. If Israel is the apple of God's eye, do you think that God will ignore any assault on Israel? Will He ignore the Holocaust, six million murdered Jews, one and a half million of whom were children? No, there will undoubtedly be judgment upon the nations. When one of the leading German, "God-is-dead" theologians, Dorothee Sölle, once said, "Since Auschwitz I cannot believe in God anymore," a rabbi responded, "Since Auschwitz I can only still believe in God, not in man anymore." One day judgment will come. As Zechariah 2:8-9 warns the nations that had plundered Israel, "...*Whoever touches you* [Israel] *touches the apple of His eye—I will surely raise My hand against them....*" In our attacks on Israel, we have not merely touched the apple of His eye; we have punched God directly in the eye, and cut the apple of His eye, His beloved people, to pieces.

> *For the Lord's portion is His people, Jacob His allotted inheritance. In a desert land He found him, in a barren and howling waste. He shielded him and cared for him; He guarded him as the apple of His eye, like an eagle that stirs up its nest and hovers over its young, that spreads its wings to catch them and carries them on its pinions. The Lord alone led him; no foreign god was with him* (Deuteronomy 32:9-12).

Chastise Israel? Yes! Destroy Israel forever? Never! "*I will not come in wrath. They will follow the Lord; He will roar like a lion. When He roars, His children will come trembling from the west*" (Hos. 11:9b-10). "Out of the west," Hosea the prophet says. It will not be from the Babylonian or Assyrian captivity, for these countries, from Israel's point of view, are to the east and the north. "*They will come trembling like birds from Egypt* [to the south, but also the land of slavery, which can be anywhere in the world], *like doves from Assyria* [thus out of the east]. *I will settle them in their homes, declares the Lord*"

(Hos. 11:11). Over the past hundred years, we have seen this happening before our very eyes.

Israel is God's firstborn son. Its very existence is miraculous, for Abraham was too old and Sarah past childbearing years when Isaac was born. God Himself gave His firstborn son life (see Gen. 17:17; 18:10-11), creating a people for His name among all the nations of the world. God's own people—through whom He would make Himself known to the whole world. Many times they were disciplined throughout their history, but abandoned and rejected? Never!

And now, Israel is returning to the land that God swore by an eternal covenant to give to them, the land of Canaan (see Ps. 105:7-11). God truly loves Israel.

ISRAEL'S RECOVERY

God speaks to His people Israel by the mouth of Isaiah the prophet:

> *Do not be afraid, for I am with you; I will bring your children from the east and gather you from the west. I will say to the north, "Give them up!" and to the south, "Do not hold them back." Bring My sons* ["*Theirs is the adoption as sons,*" says Paul in Rom. 9:4] *from afar and My daughters from the ends of the earth—everyone who is called by My name* [Israel wears God's name], *whom I created for My glory, whom I formed and made* (Isaiah 43:5-7).

Created, formed, made, and called to bear God's name—that is Israel. Isra-El, *El* meaning God. Like in Immanu-El, God with us. He brings His firstborn son back to the hills of Judea and Samaria—back to the Promised Land.

Why does He do it? Is it because Israel has become an obedient son? Does Israel see that it was God who dealt with them in history? Does Israel recognize God's great dealings with the world and with them in their own history, when God's only begotten Son came among them as a Jew, in the flesh that He received from His Jewish mother, Mary, to carry away the sins of the world, including Israel's sins?

Is it because Israel has acknowledged all these things that they are now finally allowed to return, after nearly two thousand years of "Roman" captivity? No. Israel has not (yet) become a "converted" nation. But this should be no surprise; it is exactly what the prophet Isaiah predicted would happen: *"Lead out those who have eyes but are blind, who have ears but are deaf"* (Isa. 43:8). Deaf and blind, they apparently have to be brought back to the land of Israel. Deaf to the words of the Gospel, blind to who Jesus really is. It is happening exactly as the prophet Isaiah said. Deaf and blind they would one day return to God's land. God's land? Yes, because Israel is God's land: *"The land is Mine and you are but aliens and My tenants,"* He says to Israel (Lev. 25:23b). He says, "It is My land, and I give it to you for a dwelling place."

Although for the greater part still deaf and blind to the Gospel, Israel is returning to the land. But that deafness and blindness will also change. For Paul says that *"Israel has experienced a hardening in part until the full number of the Gentiles* [the non-Jews] *has come in. And so all Israel will be saved* [How?], *as it is written: 'The Deliverer will come from Zion* [out of the heavenly Jerusalem]; *He will turn godlessness away from Jacob. And this is My covenant with them when I take away their sins'"* (Rom. 11:25b-27).

God Himself will deliver His firstborn son. He reserves that honor for Himself. And today He has started the process of Israel's redemption—the redemption of the land, the redemption of the city of Jerusalem, the redemption of the people, the redemption of the nation. The miracle of the conversion of the chosen "remnant" of Israel will be as much a miracle as any conversion is a wonder of His grace. First, Israel will be restored nationally, and then spiritually. Ezekiel says, *"For I will take you out of the nations; I will gather you from all the countries and bring you back into your own land"* (Ezek. 36:24). For decades now we have seen this happen before our very eyes. They are returning from more than 120 countries, scattered across the world.

The Lord says that when they are finally returned to the land:

> *I will sprinkle clean water on you, and you will be clean; I will cleanse you from all your impurities and from all your idols. I will give you a new heart and put a new spirit in you; I will remove from*

you your heart of stone and give you a heart of flesh. And I will put My Spirit in you and move you to follow My decrees and be careful to keep My laws. You will live in the land I gave your forefathers; you will be My people, and I will be your God (Ezekiel 36:25-28).

When Israel today returns to the Promised Land, they are there to stay. *"In that day,"* [says the Lord through Amos the prophet] *"I will restore David's fallen tent. I will repair its broken places, restore its ruins, and build it as it used to be…I will plant Israel in their own land, never again to be uprooted from the land I have given them"* (Amos 9:11,15). Never again.

Israel is on the way to her rest. *"I will come to give rest to Israel,"* says God (Jer. 31:2b). Because God really loves Israel.

GOD TRULY LOVES ISRAEL

The basis of God's relationship with Israel is love. And on the basis of this love, He made covenants with Israel, and confirmed them with an oath.

The Lord did not set His affection on you and choose you because you were more numerous than other peoples, for you were the fewest of all peoples. But it was because the Lord loved you and kept the oath He **swore** *to your forefathers that He brought you out with a mighty hand and redeemed you from the land of slavery, from the power of Pharaoh king of Egypt. Know therefore that the Lord your God is God; He is the faithful God, keeping His* **covenant of love** *to a thousand generations* (Deuteronomy 7:7-9).

Two symbolic illustrations are used to describe God's love for Israel: Father-son relationship and husband-wife relationship. Jeremiah even uses the two examples of God's relationship with Israel: Father-son and husband-wife in one breath. *"I Myself said, 'How gladly would I treat you like sons and give you a desirable land, the most beautiful inheritance of any nation. I thought you would call Me "Father" and not turn away from following Me. But like a woman unfaithful to her husband, so you have been unfaithful to Me, O house of Israel,' declares the Lord"* (Jer. 3:19-20).

Try to explain *love*! Why does a man love his wife and marry her? Because he is convinced that she is undoubtedly the most beautiful woman on earth? Or because he thinks she is the best cook ever? Or because he believes she will be the best mother for his children? Or because she is rich? Or because she is poor and he has compassion on her and falls in love with her? Or because...? No, you love her because you love her. One day that miracle happened; you saw that girl, that woman, and from then on, you did not see anyone else. If only you could be close to her, speak to her....

Rational reasons cannot explain the mystery of love. It is a gift from God "...*because God is love*" (1 John 4:8). Theologians of old used to say, "God takes reasons from within Himself. He loves because He loves. He chooses because He chooses. Always with the purpose to bless." He chose Israel to bless Israel and to make her a blessing to all the nations of the earth—to reveal Himself to the world, through His nation Israel.

> *Because He loved your forefathers and chose their descendants after them, He brought you out of Egypt by His Presence and His great strength, to drive out before you nations greater and stronger than you and to bring you into their land to give it to you for your inheritance, as it is today* (Deuteronomy 4:37-38).

> *It was not by their sword that they won the land, nor did their arm bring them victory; it was Your right hand, Your arm, and the light of Your face, for You loved them* (Psalm 44:3).

In light of the fact that God loves Israel and has elected the Jewish people for Himself, one can conclude that "love and marriage," confirmed by an oath in a covenant relationship, was and is the basis of God's relationship with Israel. He married her and pledged a solemn oath. Do you think that God will ever break an oath? No. God is a promise keeper, not a promise breaker. No matter what. And Israel is His lawful wedded wife. For better or for worse. Until death do us part, all the days of Israel's life.

Because Israel is also God's son, Israel has the right to address God as "Father."

But you are our Father, though Abraham does not know us or Israel acknowledge us; You, O Lord, are our Father, our Redeemer from of old is Your name (Isaiah 63:16).

Yet, O Lord, You are our Father… (Isaiah 64:8).

Jesus teaches His Jewish friends to pray: "…*Our Father in heaven…*" (Matt. 6:9). Israel is God's firstborn son and Jesus His only begotten Son.

The parallels between Jesus and Israel are striking.

When we read Hosea 11:1, "…*and out of Egypt I called My son,*" we as Christians might immediately think of Matthew 2:13-15: "*When they* [the magi] *had gone, an angel of the Lord appeared to Joseph in a dream. 'Get up,' he said, 'take the child and His mother and escape to Egypt. Stay there until I tell you, for Herod is going to search for the child to kill Him.' So he got up, took the child and His mother during the night and left for Egypt, where he stayed until the death of Herod. And so was fulfilled what the Lord had said through the prophet: 'Out of Egypt I called My Son.'*"

Some theologians say, "All the prophecies of the Old Testament are fulfilled in Jesus." But what does "fulfilled" mean? It means that the way of Jesus is the way of Israel, and the way of Israel is the way of Jesus. He is their greatest Son. And therefore, the way of Israel is the way of Jesus. They are totally intertwined. He is the apex of Israel. He fulfills what Israel's election is all about. He shows God's everlasting faithfulness to Israel, although election means suffering in a demon-possessed, sin-governed world. Israel's sufferings are His sufferings. Israel's escape from the bondage and slavery of Egypt by God's grace on the basis of the blood of the lambs that were slain in the houses of the Israelites typifies the freedom Jesus gives from the bondage of sin by the grace of God. There is no end to the parallels that can be drawn between the election, life, and sufferings of Jesus and the same of Israel. Jesus shows what Israel is all about. So in that sense, Jesus fulfilled *all* the prophecies. But that does not mean that many prophecies and promises regarding Israel and the Jews are not still waiting for their fulfillment as well, as some theologians claim. They are and they will be fulfilled.

Do We Know and Love the God of the Bible?

When I hear people talk negatively about Israel, even fellow-pastors or fellow-Christians, I sometimes think, *How can you say that you love God and that you love Jesus, but you apparently do not love what He loves? If you don't love Israel or you don't love the Jews, what kind of God or what kind of Jesus do you love? For God loves Israel as His firstborn son, and Jesus was a Jew. Are you really sure you love the God of the Bible, the God of Abraham, Isaac, and Jacob, the God of Israel? Or are you loving your own theological concept of God? Your theological image of God?*

Many people develop their own image of God as a god who can only act or be the way they have figured him out to be. But the Bible forbids us to worship our self-made images of God (see Exod. 20:4-6)—images in the form of wood, stone, bronze, silver, or gold, but also in the form of our own ideas about God—think-images. With all that we think or say about God, we should always use the Bible as the final examination of our own ideas. Only when we look through the eyes of God will we start to see and understand. And we can look through the eyes of God only if we listen to the Bible. Because in that Book, God has revealed Himself. We should never try to adapt God to our ideas about Him; rather, we should adapt ourselves to His ideas about us, Israel, the world around us, the past, the present, and the future.

We should always remind ourselves of the basic facts about Israel in the Bible. The relationship of God with the Jewish people and with Israel is everlasting. That alone should make us very careful when we think and talk about the Jewish people and Israel in our churches, to the media, and anyone else. We are dealing with God's people and God's land. He has never stopped loving the Jews, and He will be faithful to Himself. He will keep and fulfill all His promises to them. In the same way, whatever He has promised to the Church, He will fulfill as well. Yet we should never make an unholy theological mix of the two, as so often has happened in the history of the Church. And then came 1948.

CHAPTER TWO

The Covenants With Israel

In 1948, David Ben-Gurion declared the independent State of Israel. The astonished world then saw the Lord God, as in Old Testament times, fight for His people Israel against overpowering enemies who again and again, in 1948, 1956, 1967, and 1973, set out to destroy Israel. And the centuries-old, theological house of cards that the Church had built collapsed. The Church was confronted with many questions, such as:

- ❖ Is the return of Israel to their land a fulfillment of biblical prophecy?

- ❖ Is God still involved with the Jewish people, with Israel?

- ❖ Is the covenant with Abraham and Isaac and Jacob, and with Moses and Joshua, still valid? Does the Lord still remain faithful to those covenants?

- ❖ Where does that leave us, the Christian Church?

- ❖ What is our position with God?

❖ Because isn't it true that for the most part, Israel still does not believe in Jesus? So how can the Lord still bless them? How does it all fit together?

❖ What is the connection between the old and the new covenants, between the Old and the New Testaments? Are there two covenants that remain simultaneously in effect? Are there two peoples of God?

❖ What is God's relationship with Israel? And to us?

Questions like these continue to confront and challenge the Church and many theologians.

A Land, a People, and a Blessing

It all started with the calling of *Abraham* in Genesis 12:1-3.

God made a basic covenant with this forefather of Israel, which is the cornerstone of all other covenants. Indeed, all other covenants with Israel are an enlargement of this covenant.

> *The Lord had said to Abram, "Leave your country, your people and your father's household and go to the land I will show you. I will make you into a great nation and I will bless you; I will make your name great, and you will be a blessing. I will bless those who bless you, and whoever curses you I will curse; and all peoples on earth will be blessed through you"* (Genesis 12:1-3).

Seven times God uses the formula "I will," either expressed or understood! The three basic elements of this Abrahamic covenant are a land, a nation/people, and a blessing—a blessing for Abraham himself, for Israel, and through Abraham for all nations/peoples on earth.

Sometimes people think that this was a promise just for Abraham personally, and had nothing to do with the people or nation of Israel. They claim, "God said that whosoever would bless Abraham personally during his lifetime would be blessed, and whoever would curse Abraham would be cursed. But that has nothing to do with Israel or the Jewish people as such." Comparing Scripture with Scripture though, we read in Numbers 23:8-10:

> *How can I curse those whom God has not cursed? How can I denounce those whom the Lord has not denounced? From the rocky peaks I see them, from the heights I view them. I see a people who live apart and do not consider themselves one of the nations [Lo, the people shall dwell alone, and shall not be reckoned among the nations—KJV]. Who can count the dust of Jacob or number the fourth part of Israel? Let me die the death of the righteous, and may my end be like theirs!*

Here was a man, Balaam, hired to curse the people of Israel when they were wandering in the desert, on their way from Egypt to the Promised Land. From the mountaintops he looked at them, and then he said that he simply could not curse those who God had not cursed. Later, he concluded in Numbers 24:9, *"Like a lion they crouch and lie down, like a lioness—who dares to rouse them? 'May those who bless you be blessed and those who curse you be cursed!'"* So, Balaam applied the promise of God of blessing or cursing to the whole nation/people of Israel, not just to Abraham personally.

The Lord confirmed this Abrahamic covenant with Isaac in Genesis 26:1-5;23-24.

The Lord again confirmed this Abrahamic covenant with Jacob in Genesis 28:3-4;13-15 and Genesis 35:9-13.

Therefore, the Bible calls Him "the God of Abraham, Isaac, and Jacob" (see Exod. 3:6). That is one of His names. The lines of Ishmael (also a son of Abraham) and Esau (the twin brother of Jacob) are cut off from the line of the Abrahamic covenant, although there are great blessings for Ishmael and his descendants. The covenant line continues after Jacob through the 12 sons or the 12 tribes of Jacob (see Gen. 49).

CONDITIONAL AND UNCONDITIONAL

Unconditional covenants are those in which God promises to do certain things, no matter what. What He will do is not dependent upon the behavior of the other partner(s) in these covenants. God simply states that this is what He is going to do, because He has made this decision for reasons of His own.

Whereas, in conditional covenants, the Lord promises to do something only if the other partner(s) keep their side of the covenant or contract, meeting and fulfilling their obligations.

There are six unconditional covenants.

1. The Abrahamic covenant (see Gen. 12:1-3).

2. The covenant of the Promised Land, or the land of Israel covenant, or the land of Canaan covenant (see Gen. 12:1; 13:14-17; 15:18-21; Deut. 30:1-10; Ps. 105:7-11).

3. The Levitical covenant (see Num. 25:10-13; Neh. 13:29; Jer. 33:19-23; Mal. 2:1-9).

4. The Davidic covenant (see 2 Sam. 7:10-16; Ps. 89; Ezek. 37:24-25).

5. The new covenant (see Jer. 31:31-34).

6. The Jerusalem covenant (see Ezek. 16).

There is one conditional covenant.

1. The covenant of the Law, the covenant of Sinai, the Mosaic covenant, the "old" covenant (see Exod. 19:5; 20:1-17; Deut. 5). Deuteronomy 28 contains the two-part formula of this covenant. Verses 1-14 describe the first part, "If you will…then I will bless," and verses 15-68 reveal the second part, "If you do not…then I will curse." One has to meet certain requirements in order to obtain the blessings of the covenant of the Law. This covenant was renewed on the plains of Moab (see Deut. 29:1-15), at Mounts Ebal

and Gerizim (see Josh. 8:30-35), and at Shechem (see Josh. 24). This covenant of the Law is the "old" covenant. Paul discusses the difference between the "old" and the "new" covenant in his Epistle to the Hebrews: *"By calling this covenant 'new,' He has made the first one* [the 'old' one, the covenant of the Law] *obsolete; and what is obsolete and aging will soon disappear"* (Heb. 8:13).

EVERLASTING

The covenants are to be taken literally, as a contract between two parties. And these covenants are eternal, everlasting, and made with Israel that will therefore exist forever. And because these covenants are in place forever, God cannot change His mind about them.

- ❖ The Abrahamic covenant (see Gen. 17:7,13,19).

- ❖ The land of Israel/Canaan covenant (see 1 Chron. 16:17-18; Ps. 105:10).

- ❖ The Levitical covenant (see Num. 25:10-13; Jer. 33:19-23; Mal. 2:1-9).

- ❖ The Davidic covenant (see 2 Sam. 23:5; 1 Chron. 17:11-14; Ps. 89:19-29; Isa. 55:3; Ezek. 37:24-25).

- ❖ The new covenant (see Jer. 31:31-34; Isa. 61:7-9; Jer. 50:5; Heb. 13:20; Jer. 32:37-41). We read a lot about the (sinful) heart and soul of man in the Bible, but this is, as far as I know, the only place in Scripture that talks about the heart and soul of God. God is very excited about bringing the Jewish people back to the Promised Land!

- ❖ The Jerusalem covenant (see Ezek. 16:59-60;62; Isa. 4:2-5). At the beginning of Ezekiel chapter 16, the Lord addresses Jerusalem, but He is not simply talking to bricks, mortar, and Jerusalem stone; He is speaking collectively to "Zion"—the city, the land, and the people—the divinely ordered unity. This "marriage covenant" with Jerusalem encompasses most other covenants—the Abrahamic covenant, the covenant of the Law, the land covenant, the Davidic covenant, and ultimately the new covenant.

The shekhinah glory of the Lord dwelt in the temple that was built by King Solomon (see 2 Chron. 7:1-2); then Ezekiel saw the shekhinah glory of the Lord depart from the temple shortly before the Babylonians destroyed it (see Ezek. 10:3-5; 11:22-23); and it will return to the temple as the permanent return of the presence of the Lord, the God of Israel, takes place, to dwell among His ancient covenant people (see Ezek. 43:1-2;4-7a). The Book of Revelation tells us that the earthly reign of Messiah in Jerusalem will last a thousand years (see Rev. 20:4-5). As the only place in the Bible where a time limit is placed on the Messianic Age on planet Earth, it seems to be at odds with most of the prophecies in the Bible concerning the Messianic Kingdom, which emphatically tell us that it will be an everlasting Kingdom. And so it will be. Only the theater of the Messianic Kingdom will be moved from one stage to another.

The Jerusalem covenant goes so far as to link the earthly city with the heavenly city (see Isa. 65:17-19; Rev. 21). Isaiah tells us here that in the New Jerusalem there will be no memory of the horror surrounding or associated with the previous city and the world in which it existed. The new heavens and the new earth will become the place of the eternal Messianic Kingdom. Just as the Abrahamic covenant promises the land of Israel and the earthly Jerusalem as the inheritance for all Jewish people for all times, whether they are living in the land or in the diaspora, the New Testament promises the heavenly Jerusalem as the eternal inheritance for those whose names are written in the Lamb's Book of Life (see Heb. 12:22-24; 13:14). That includes all those who partake of the new covenant, whether they are Jew or Gentile.

CHAPTER THREE

The Judgment of Innocent Bloodshed

Many people who have had a Christian upbringing, as I did, were probably taught about Israel and the Jewish people in the same way I was taught. Teachers in a Christian school, a Sunday school, in a catechism class, or maybe even at home would say, "The Old Testament, the first part of the Bible, deals with the old covenant God made with Israel; the New Testament, the second part of the Bible, deals with God's new covenant made with Christians, with the Church."

One is given the impression that Israel had been God's chosen people until the moment they said "no" to Jesus. And then their place was taken by this new people of God, all those who believe in Jesus. The "new Israel," they proclaim them to be. The spiritual Israel. This new people of God, the Church, is made up of everyone who believes in Jesus, whether Jew or Gentile, Dutch or Chinese, white or brown or black, rich or poor, young or old, man or woman (see Eph. 2:11-21). Everyone who believes in Jesus is welcome.

And all that is true, of course, but almost automatically the thought arises that the Jewish people, Israel, have ceased to be the chosen people of

God, that God has rejected His firstborn son. The Church has said, "They [the Jews] rejected Jesus and are therefore no longer God's chosen people. And yes, it is very sad, but if you want to know what happens to people who turn against God and His Anointed One, then take a look at the Jewish people. It is awful—all those centuries of persecution of the Jews— but after all, they murdered Jesus and are now being punished by God. Didn't they themselves say, *'Let His blood be on us and on our children'* (Matt. 27:25b)? Yes, it's all very sad—what has happened to the Jews; but isn't it their own fault? Certainly, it is the judgment of God, and it's a warning to us all!"

This is how many Christian people have talked and thought, and still do today!

God is not particularly involved with the Jewish people, they say, except as they receive His punishments and judgments, while the Christian Church now receives His rich blessings. "Just look," they say, "at how the Church has grown since the time when Constantine made Christianity the official religion of the Roman Empire. It has rolled back the Roman Empire from within and pushed heathen darkness further and further away in Europe. Christian civilizations have sprung up in the countries of Western and Eastern Europe, in Russia and America, in Australia and Africa, and wherever missionaries have gone."

And all this is certainly true.

IT WAS NOT THE JEWS

And Israel?

The "wandering Jew" (blind, craving for money, always deceitful and hungry for power, as many people have claimed or thought, and some still do today) became a hunted being. The Christian Church conveniently forgot that she herself had forced the Jews into money-lending in the Middle Ages and labeled it a godless business, not to be entered into by respectable Christian people. The Church forgot that she herself had prevented Jews from belonging to trade guilds and taking up ordinary occupations and jobs. And what about the Jews' so-called thirst for power? If you follow the struggles for power between Christian kings and popes, landowners and nobility, trades-men and farmers, citizens and cloisters, through the ages in all European countries, you get a good impression of what the words "power hungry" mean. But time after time the Jews were robbed, hunted, raped, separated out, and herded into ghettos, before finally being carried off to the concentra-tion camps. A systematic attempt was made to murder every Jew. Great and small, from the oldest to the youngest, they were to be gassed and the corpses burned in the crematoria.

Persecuting Jews was even considered by the Church to be a God-pleasing work; for after all, were the Jews not the murderers of Jesus? It was conve-niently forgotten that in reality, the Jews did not murder Jesus, but that the non-Jews, the Romans, did so. The Jews were not even sufficiently masters in their own land to be allowed to carry out the death penalty. The Romans were in charge. Whenever Jewish law courts imposed a death penalty, they had to ask permission from the Roman procurator—in this case, Pontius Pilate; and if he granted their petition, the sentence was carried out by Roman soldiers.

Such was the case with Jesus. The Jews sentenced Him to death and the non-Jews, the Romans, crucified Him when they carried out the death sen-tence approved and pronounced by Pontius Pilate. Was Pontius Pilate put under severe pressure to do what the Jews wanted? Certainly. But still the final responsibility was on his shoulders. And he was not a man to be easily intimidated. On other occasions, he had simply sent in the troops, creating a bloodbath by massacring hundreds of Jews (see Luke 13:1). But in this case, he didn't mind giving these complaining Jews what they asked for. And one can wash one's hands in innocence, but Pontius Pilate was the Roman procurator, and no washing of hands could remove that responsibility. This is why Pontius Pilate is explicitly mentioned in the Apostles' Creed, which originated in the early Christian Church: "He suffered under Pontius Pilate, was crucified, dead, and buried." The old Church still knew who was re-sponsible. Thus, it is even historically incorrect to say that it was the Jews who murdered Jesus.

The apostle John, who stood at the cross and watched the Roman soldiers pierce Jesus' hands and feet with nails, and finally pierce His side with the spear, said: *"These things happened so that the scripture would be fulfilled:... 'They will look on the one they have pierced'"* (John 19:36-37).

Who did the piercing? The Romans did. Who did the looking? The Jews did.

If one wishes to talk about who is guilty of the death of Jesus, the answer is that we all are guilty. It is as if we, each one personally, spoke the death sentence and handled the hammer, the nails, and the spear. Because *"He was pierced for our transgressions, He was crushed for our iniquities; the punishment that brought us peace was upon Him, and by His wounds we are healed"* (Isa. 53:5). Our sins brought Him to the cross. He was and is the Lamb of God who takes away the sins of the world (see John 1:29,36). He Himself said, *"No one takes it* [My life] *from Me, but I lay it down of My own accord"* (John 10:18a). The 17th-century Dutch poet Jacobus Revius expresses this beautifully in his poem.

HE CARRIED OUR AFFLICTIONS

It's not the Jews, Lord Jesus, who crucified You,
Nor those who betrayed You before the court,
Nor those who gleefully spat in Your face,
Nor those who beat You and bruised You,
It's not the soldiers with their hard-balled fists,
Who placed the thorns or lifted the hammer,
Or raised the cursed wood on Golgotha,
Or gambled and fought over Your garments:
It is I, O Lord, I am the one who did this,
I am the heavy tree that You carried,
I am the strong rope with which You were tied,
The nails, and the spear, the whip that scourged You,
The blood-bespattered crown, You wore on Your head,
Because all this happened, alas (!) for my sins.

The Judgment of Innocent Bloodshed

For centuries, Christendom has maintained that the Jewish people, Israel, killed Christ. and that consequently, God's judgment rests on them. We, the Church, have declared ourselves the new people of God, and if Jews wish to join us, they must, like everyone else, come to faith in Jesus, be baptized, and in effect, stop being Jews. But does a man cease to be a man, or a woman cease to be a woman (see Gal. 3:26-29), or a Chinese cease to be Chinese when they come to faith? And yet we expect a Jew to stop being a Jew when he comes to faith in Jesus? And furthermore, the Church has determined that if Jews do not do this, and do not believe in Jesus, then God's judgment will continue to rest upon them (see John 3:36). Incredibly, the Christian Church has actually often helped to implement "God's judgment" on the Jews.

"HIS BLOOD BE ON US"

One of the verses that has been misused throughout the ages by the Church to teach that Israel has been rejected and is under a perpetuating curse and judgment of God, is Matthew 27:25b: *"Let His blood be on us and on our children."* (Perhaps the background for this expression can be found in Ezekiel 3:16-21.)

It is this verse, this terrible cry shouted by the crowd in Jerusalem, that is often quoted to defend the view that Israel's tragic fate throughout history is her own fault. Many have said, "Yes, it is terrible—all that has happened throughout the centuries to the Jews. But let's face it—didn't they more or less ask for it when they killed Jesus? Isn't it a warning to us all? Isn't this what happens to people who reject the Lord and His Anointed One? Isn't this the judgment of God?" And the Church over the centuries has even "helped" to bring this judgment of God about, by developing a Christian theology that can be labeled as Christian anti-Semitism and by inciting hatred and creating an anti-Jewish atmosphere in which terrible persecutions of Jews can happen, notwithstanding the fact that some Christians have personally behaved decently and have tried to help the Jews as much as they can. So, let us look at this Bible verse a little closer and more carefully in order not to jump to any wrong conclusions too quickly.

Many Christians believe, as I do, that the Bible is God's Word, totally trustworthy and reliable, and that one should consider the literal meaning of the
words first and accept and believe them, before you start looking for spiritual
meanings and interpretations. We should not spiritualize or allegorize God's
Word, although we can always draw spiritual lessons from it. Having said this,
at least seven conclusions can be drawn when considering this Scripture.

1. Perhaps a few hundred Jews, inflamed by some of their religious leaders, stood in front of the house of Pontius Pilate and shouted, *"His
   blood be on us and on our children."* Jesus was apparently very popular,
   even among the Jerusalemites. Why otherwise would they have ar-
   rested Him at night? (see Mark 14:2; Luke 22:6). The people living in
   the north of Israel didn't have a clue as to what was happening in
   Jerusalem, and many of them would undoubtedly have disapproved—
   if they only had known. Can one hold the whole of the Jewish people
   responsible, then and now, for what this small mob in Jerusalem did,
   incited by some of their religious leaders, asking for His crucifixion?
   The Church has done just that, and shoved the guilt for the death of
   Jesus into the "shoes of the Jews." This is demonical, and it has led to
   the spilling of rivers of Jewish blood in the lands of Christendom. But
   there is more to it.

2. If we apply the principle of first considering the literal meaning of
   Bible verses, then we must conclude that these terrible words have
   already been fulfilled. The phrase, *"...us and our children"* that this
   group of Jews shouted, was meant for their own particular generation, and their children—the next generation of these Jerusalemites.
   Subsequently, the Jews who shouted these words, and their children, were murdered 40 years later by the Romans, in Jerusalem.

   One of the biblical numbers for the duration of one generation is 40,
   referring to the duration of the wandering in the desert where the
   generation who left Egypt died because of their unbelief. Another is
   70, spanning the time of a grandfather to his grandson—*"...from
   generation to generation..."* (see Dan. 4:3,34). And another is 100

(see Gen. 15:13,16). In A.D. 70, Titus and his legions razed the city and the temple to the ground, murdering 1,100,000 Jews (according to the Jewish historian of those days, Flavius Josephus), and crucifying thousands from Jerusalem to the coast of the Mediterranean Sea, until there was not enough wood left to construct more crosses. And in A.D. 135, Emperor Hadrian finished the job by quenching the revolt under Simon Bar Kokhba in three years, killing another 600,000 Jews, in addition to those who died, of hunger, disease, and fire (according to the Roman historian in those days, Dio Cassius).

Were these the moments that His blood "came on" that same generation and their children, the next generation? Taking into account that these massacres happened 40 and 100 years after Jesus' crucifixion around A.D. 30, we realize that this prophecy has already been fulfilled—if one considers the words "*us and our children*" in their first and literal meaning. Moreover, all other Jewish blood that has been spilled over the centuries ever since has had nothing to do with God's judgment, but instead, are terrible sins, crimes of men, waiting for God's final judgment.

3. But this leads to another question. Did the Romans actually bring God's judgment upon these Jewish people—them and their children? Was this *God's* judgment? Does God judge in such a way? Indeed, 40 years later, the Roman legions captured and destroyed Jerusalem and the temple, and brutally murdered that generation and their children. However, among them were undoubtedly also thousands of *Jewish Christians*! If this Scripture, "*us and our children*," means that the small Jewish crowd with some of their leaders in Jerusalem were taking responsibility for the death of Jesus, would God also include Jewish Christians in such a "judgment"? The question whether all the Christian Jews had fled to Pella before the siege of Jerusalem, is still an issue hotly debated by historians. Some say that there was no such flight! So among the many victims of the atrocities of the Roman legions there could well have been many

Jewish Christians and some Gentile Christians, as well as Jews in Jerusalem who had not even participated in the mob who was shouting and yelling before Pontius Pilate demanding Jesus' crucifixion. Did they deserve God's judgment? Hence, we have another reason to ask the question: Was this destruction of the inhabitants of Jerusalem in A.D. 70 actually a "judgment of God"?

4. A lot of innocent Jewish blood has been spilled since then, throughout the centuries, in the lands of Christendom in Europe, in Islamic nations, and elsewhere in the world. All this innocent blood, since the death and resurrection of Jesus, is now awaiting God's revenge at the Last Judgment. Or is all of the innocent blood—Jewish and non-Jewish—of the last 2000 years and more, still calling from the earth? And is it all awaiting the judgment of God at the end of time? Innocent blood like that of Zechariah, the son of Berekiah— "*And so upon you* [at the time of the final judgment?] *will come all the righteous blood that has been shed on earth, from the blood of righteous Abel to the blood of Zechariah son of Berekiah, whom you murdered between the temple and the altar*" (Matt. 23:35)?

Is there a difference between "innocent blood" before Christ and "innocent blood" after Christ? Has God's judgment on the innocent blood of Zechariah, the son of Berekiah, spilled by some Jews centuries before Christ, already come to pass in the terrible destruction of Jerusalem in A.D. 70? Does God have a special judgment for Jews in the case of "spilled blood"? Or does all innocent blood on the earth of all the centuries of human history—Jewish and non-Jewish innocent blood, including that of Zechariah the son of Berekiah, wait for the revenge one day by God Almighty in the final day of His wrath, at the end of times? Indeed, we must also consider the blood of Abel that was shed of which Jesus speaks; it was shed long before the Jewish people were even in existence, even before Abraham, even before the flood!

5. And who is the One who will finally take "revenge"? Who will bring judgment? Man or God? Can Romans bring God's judgment on Israel? Can people execute God's judgment? Paul says in Romans 12:19, "*Do not take revenge, my friends, but leave room for God's wrath, for it is written: 'It is Mine to avenge; I will repay,' says the Lord.*" God will one day "avenge" the wrongdoings of man and all the spilling of innocent blood. Consider the innocent blood of the Christian martyrs in Revelation 6:9-11: "*When He opened the fifth seal, I saw under the altar the souls of those who had been slain because of the word of God and the testimony they had maintained. They called out in a loud voice, 'How long, Sovereign Lord, holy and true, until You judge the inhabitants of the earth and avenge our blood?' Then each of them was given a white robe, and they were told to wait a little longer, until the number of their fellow servants and brothers who were to be killed as they had been was completed.*"

One day God will finally sit in judgment to avenge all the innocent blood that was ever spilled on this earth, including the innocent blood of all victims of violence, the millions murdered in the womb by abortionists, the victims of rape, of incest, the exploited ones, the slaves. He will judge the torturers and the murderers, the dictators and the exploiters, Romans, Germans, Dutch, Chinese, Russians, Americans, Spanish, British, Arab, Palestinian, Jewish, and of whatever race, cultural, religious, or philosophical background the perpetrators are, have been, or will be. About this final judgment, John says in Revelation 21:8, "*…This is the second death.*" And Paul informs us in Galatians 5:21b, "*I warn you, as I did before, that those who live like this will not inherit the kingdom of God*" (see also verses 19-21a).

The conclusion must be: all the sins of men—Jews and non-Jews alike—await God's judgment at the end of time. He is to be the Judge. Men can never execute God's judgment. Everyone awaits the final verdict at the end of time, and until that time there is only One who has been punished and has felt God's judgment on behalf of us all—Jesus. The Bible says that whosoever puts his or her faith in Him will never come into God's final judgment. So, the destruction of Jerusalem and the land of Israel by the Romans in A.D. 70 and A.D. 135 was probably not a judgment of God at all, but crimes committed by the Romans who will be held accountable for them in the final day of God's judgment.

6. Perhaps there is quite a different interpretation for this exclamation of the yelling crowd. Could the cry of that mob in Jerusalem have been an unconscious and unintentional prophetic truth being uttered, as was the case with Caiaphas quoted in John 11:49-50: *"Then one of them, named Caiaphas, who was high priest that year, spoke up, 'You know nothing at all! You do not realize that it is better for you that one man die for the people than that the whole nation perish'"*? Caiaphas did not understand the full implication of what he was saying, and he surely did not mean those words to be prophetic in the sense that John understood them. But it still was very true. Jesus, the "one man," died to redeem many people and save them. One man died instead of the whole nation or, for that matter, the whole of mankind.

God in His grace found and executed this incredible solution to the problem of the sin of man. And the Son cooperated wholeheartedly with the loving purposes of His merciful Father, and made His life available to become the blameless Lamb who would be slaughtered for the sins of the world. In John 11:51-52 concerning Caiaphas' words, John explains: *"He did not say this on his own, but as high priest that year he prophesied that Jesus would die for the Jewish nation, and not only for that nation but also for the scattered children of God, to bring them together and make them one."*

Could the cry *"His blood be on us and on our children"* work in a similar fashion—as an unintentionally uttered phrase, but nevertheless a deep, spiritual, and prophetic truth? Surely, the blood of Jesus was to come upon us and cleanse us from all our sins. The blood of Jesus must also come upon Israel to cleanse Israel's sins. Of course, what they meant was to take upon themselves the responsibility for the death of Jesus. So their cry was not an honest sinner's prayer, but nevertheless they did speak a deep truth, even if it was unintentional. This leads to the final, and in my opinion, decisive point.

7. On the cross Jesus prayed, *"…Father, forgive them, for they do not know what they are doing"* (Luke 23:34a). When He was praying this prayer upon the cross, Jesus as the Lamb of God was giving His blood to redeem the sins of the world right then and there—to make it possible for God to forgive our sins. Would the Father not answer the prayer of His dying Son for all those who were directly involved in His execution? Surely He forgave the Roman soldiers and the yelling Jewish crowd, and Pontius Pilate and Herod, and the Sanhedrin and all the people involved in the process of condemning and killing Him. For they indeed did not know what they were doing. The Sanhedrin, Pontius Pilate, and Herod had no clue what was going on or what was really happening.

Peter says in Acts 3:17-18: *"Now, brothers, I know that you acted in ignorance, as did your leaders. But this is how God fulfilled what He had foretold through all the prophets, saying that His Christ would suffer."* The Lamb of God had to be slain in order for the sins of the world to be forgiven. John the Baptist immediately recognized this great commission of Jesus when he saw Him coming toward him. *"The next day John saw Jesus coming toward him and said, 'Look, the Lamb of God, who takes away the sin of the world!'"* (John 1:29). *"The next day John was there again with two of his disciples. When he saw Jesus passing by, he said, 'Look, the Lamb of God!'"* (John 1:35-36).

Furthermore, Jesus was not murdered by accident, or against His will. For He said, *"No one takes it [My life] from Me, but I lay it down of My own accord. I have authority to lay it down and authority to take it up again"* (John 10:18; see also Matt. 20:28). He came into this world, to give His life as a free offering for the sins of the world—to be slaughtered as a Lamb. Isaiah prophesied about Him in chapter 53:

> *Surely He took up our infirmities and carried our sorrows, yet we considered Him stricken by God, smitten by Him, and afflicted. But He was pierced for our transgressions, He was crushed for our iniquities; the punishment that brought us peace was upon Him, and by His wounds we are healed…He was led like a lamb to the slaughter, and as a sheep before her shearers is silent, so He did not open His mouth…He was cut off from the land of the living; for the transgression of My people He was stricken…though He had done no violence, nor was any deceit in His mouth. Yet it was the Lord's will to crush Him and cause Him to suffer…He poured out His life unto death, and was numbered with the transgressors. For He bore the sin of many, and made intercession for the transgressors"* (Isaiah 53:4-5,7-10,12).

So, the prayer of Jesus on the cross ended the curse that this Jewish mob invoked upon themselves right there. And all the innocent Jewish blood that has been spilled throughout the ages still waits for God's judgment and revenge at the end of time.

The Church needs to confess its guilt for this almost diabolical theology over the centuries that has led to the shedding of rivers of Jewish blood and agelong Christian anti-Semitism, before it is too late and she is held responsible before the throne of God. We as Christians should personally look into our minds, hearts, and souls to determine whether there is any hidden Christian anti-Semitism as well, for which God will ultimately hold us responsible.

CHAPTER FOUR

A New Covenant

With whom have all covenants in the Bible been actually made? It might come as a shock to us Christians, but all covenants since Abraham have been made with Israel alone. There is not one covenant that has been made with the Church. Praise the Lord, however, one of the covenants made with Israel has also been opened to non-Jews who are allowed to become partakers with Israel. This is the new covenant.

We have been told by some theologians that the old covenant has been made with Israel and the new covenant has been made with the Church. How remarkable, then, that Paul, speaking about Israel (his brothers after the flesh, the Jews) and summarizing all their blessings, says that "theirs are the covenants" (see Rom. 9:4)—plural! Not just the (old) covenant, but the "*covenants*" (plural), indicating both the old and the new covenant, and some other covenants as well!

Where did he get this idea? From Jeremiah 31:31-34, where the prophet says:

"The time is coming," declares the Lord, *"when I will make a new covenant* [With whom? With the Church? No!] *with the house of Israel and with the house of Judah. It will not be like the covenant I made with their forefathers when I took them by the hand to lead them out of Egypt* [the covenant of the law], *because they broke My covenant, though I was a husband to them,"* declares the Lord. *"This is the covenant I will make with the house of Israel after that time,"* declares the Lord. *"I will put My law in their minds and write it on their hearts. I will be their God, and they will be My people. No longer will a man teach his neighbor, or a man his brother, saying, 'Know the Lord,' because they will all know Me, from the least of them to the greatest,"* declares the Lord. *"For I will forgive their wickedness and will remember their sins no more."*

So the new covenant was to be made one day with Israel!

FIRST THE JEW, AND THEN THE GENTILE

When was this new covenant with the house of Israel and with the house of Judah made? Or does it still have to be made with the Jewish people, as some people think? Is this still "music of the future" for Israel?

Let us look at the Lord Jesus' own words at the Last Supper: *"He took bread, gave thanks and broke it, and gave it to them, saying, 'This is My body given for you; do this in remembrance of Me.' In the same way, after the supper He took the cup, saying, 'This cup is* [what?] *the new covenant in My blood, which is poured out for you'"* (Luke 22:19-20). The Lord Jesus, a flesh-and-blood Jew, surrounded by His Jewish disciples, pointed to the signs of the new covenant. There was not a single Gentile in sight. At that moment, He was establishing the new covenant with Israel; His broken body and His poured-out blood were the signs of the new covenant, which spoke of redemption and forgiveness of the sins of the world, the sins of Jews and non-Jews alike.

It is important to note that everything up to this point had been a totally inner-Jewish affair. Later, at the Feast of Pentecost, only Jews and proselytes (non-Jews who had converted to Judaism and thus had become Jews) were present in Jerusalem when the Holy Spirit was poured out (see Acts 2:11). Just as the Last Supper, Pentecost in Jerusalem was also a totally inner-Jewish affair. But what about us? When did we Gentiles come in? We had to wait until Acts chapter 10. Then the Gentile Roman centurion, Cornelius, to the utter amazement of the circumcised believers and even to Peter himself, saw the Holy Spirit poured out upon the heathens (see Acts 10:44-47). Upon Gentiles! Non-Jews! From that moment on, non-Jews were added to the new covenant, and the new covenant was opened up for them.

Later, Paul started to grasp what had happened there at the house of Cornelius; and since then, everywhere among the Gentiles, whenever the Gospel was preached, people received Jesus as their Lord and Savior. These people were like new branches being grafted onto the old root (see Rom. 11:24), into the new covenant with Israel. They were cut off from their Gentile roots and grafted onto the new root. What a difference it would have made if Romans chapter 11 had been read carefully and preached in the Church.

We are engrafted. We are not at the core; rather, the Jews are. The Church has said, "The Jews must come to us. They have to convert to Jesus, and then they more or less lose their Jewishness. Then they become part of the Church and become Christians, just like all of us." But the truth is just the opposite. They do not have to come to us, to the Church; instead, by the grace of God, we are added to them—into their new covenant—engrafted. Be careful, as Paul warns the Gentile Christian believers; you do not carry the root, but the root carries you (see Rom. 11:18). By God's grace, you Gentiles are permitted to share in their new covenant. Isn't that wonderful?

So now, God is our covenant God as well! We are engrafted into a new covenant. He will be faithful, despite our unfaithfulness. He is a God who elects. If He can be faithful toward a disobedient Israel and keep His promises to them, He can and will be faithful to His so-often disobedient Church and keep His promises to her as well. And He can be and will be faithful to an often disobedient "me." There is hope for you and me! Despite our unfaithfulness and disobedience, He looks upon us in Jesus, whose broken body and spilled blood are the signs of the new covenant. The Lord even hardened and blinded 99 percent of Israel, deciding to not yet give them revelation about Jesus, while letting us in first!

But someday in the future, God will do this for "all Israel" as well. He used the prophet Jeremiah to announce that the new covenant would be for the house of Israel and the house of Judah. Paul is clear that once God's work of grace among the Gentiles has been completed, He will save "all Israel." Then the Deliverer will come from Zion, and He Himself will turn ungodliness away from Jacob and take away their sins (see Rom. 11:25-27). Paul says to us: Be glad, therefore, Gentiles, that God for a time, has set aside His own Jewish people (branches were broken off) in order that you might be grafted in (see Rom. 11:19-20). But He will continue to be with Israel, He will reattach the broken-off, natural branches to the olive tree, because He is faithful to Himself and to His covenant(s).

Christian Church, and Christian community, do not be arrogant, but fear! Be astounded at the grace of God toward you. Note that He will remember His grace and will never neglect His faithfulness with regard to Israel. For the Jewish people are coming home! Israel is reborn as a nation! And that means that the Savior is on His way! In His own way and in His own time, He will reveal Himself to His Jewish brothers.

JOSEPH

Let us look for a moment at the story of Joseph and his brothers. Before Joseph revealed himself to his brothers who had come to him in Egypt to ask for food because there was a famine in Israel, and who had not recognized Joseph as their brother, he did a remarkable thing. He sent the Egyptians, the non-Jews, the Gentiles, out of the room. This was none of their business (see Gen. 45:1). And only after they had left did Joseph descend from his throne and say, "I am Joseph!" "It is really me!" (see Gen. 45:3). To me this is a beautiful illustration of how Jesus will finally be recognized by His Jewish brothers and sisters.

Until that moment, Joseph's brothers had not recognized him. He spoke in a foreign Egyptian tongue, not Hebrew, even as the New Testament is written in Greek and not in Hebrew. He did not look like a Jew; his clothes and hair were those of an Egyptian noble just as Jesus is often portrayed in many paintings as anything but Jewish. In fact, He sometimes looks more like a Greek Apollo than a Jew! Joseph might even have been adored by the Egyptians as a god in their temples. Why? Joseph was elevated to such a high position that he probably was considered one of Pharaoh's sons (see Gen. 41:39-45). The Pharaoh was considered to be the sun god and was worshipped as a god by the Egyptians. Accordingly, his sons were sometimes considered to be rays of that blazing sun god. The entire family had at least a touch of divinity about them. Similarly, Jesus is worshipped as a God by many in Christian churches and is adored and prayed to by many at statues in different churches (temples) all over the world, which is abhorrent to Jews!

How often through the centuries has the Church misrepresented Jesus to the Jews. Sometimes, Jews are convinced that we, like the Egyptians, have more than one god—the Father is God, Jesus is God, and the Holy Spirit is God; and some of us also seem to have a goddess by the name of Mary, because some Christians pray to her too. But the time will come when Israel will see who Jesus really is, similar to the story of Joseph. His brothers did not recognize him as their brother when he was all-powerful among the Gentiles, and that situation lingered on until Joseph decided to make himself known to his brothers.

Then Joseph said a peculiar thing to the Egyptians. "Could you please leave the room for a minute? This is between me and my brothers." And after they had left the room, he came down from his throne and said, "I am Joseph, your brother. It is really me. And it has been me all the time." At that point, they probably embraced each other and perhaps shed some tears.

One day, Jesus will reveal Himself to the Jews, and then they will hug and shed some tears, just like the brothers of Joseph did (see Gen. 45:2). In His time and in His own way, God will do it: *I will come to give rest to Israel*" (Jer. 31:2b). What a great time of reconciliation that will be—between Him and His brothers! No Gentiles will be involved in that moment. This is clear from God's repeated "I wills" in Jeremiah 31:31–35 (quoted by Paul in Romans 11:26–27):

"I will...I will...I will..." says the sovereign Lord. He will come from Zion and take away their sins. He Himself will do so for the last generation of Israel, for the remnant who will have returned to the land of Israel.

JEWS KNOW GOD

"But," some say, "what happens to Jews who have died without believing in Jesus? Are they saved or are they eternally lost?" I reply, "I want to tell you a story that a Jewish friend passed on to me."

During the Second World War, when he was 11 years old, my friend and other Jewish children were led into a remote Polish forest, to a place where a deep trench had been dug and soldiers were standing ready with machine guns. The boy broke away from the group of children and hurried into the thick bushes. From a safe distance, hidden behind a tree, he watched to see what would happen. When the children arrived at the edge of the trench, the rabbi who was accompanying them made a request: "May I sing and pray with the children?" The request was granted. Then the children, along with the rabbi, sang, *"The Lord is my Shepherd, I shall not want."* And they continued with the beautiful words of the Twenty-third Psalm that have over the ages been such a comfort to so many people, Jew and Christian, on their deathbeds. *"Even though I walk through the valley of the shadow of death, I will fear no evil, for You are with me; Your rod and Your staff* [belonging to a shepherd], *they comfort me"* (Ps. 23:4). I lack nothing because the Lord is my shepherd.

None of the children, nor the rabbi, knew of or believed in the Lord Jesus as the Good Shepherd. However, they went into eternity with the words of their own Jewish Psalms, from their Word of God, on their lips. We often tend to forget that the Psalms are Jewish; they are the Psalms of Israel. Instead, we incorrectly think they are Christian songs. These Jewish children and their rabbi went into eternity with the words of the eternal God on their lips, the God who revealed these words to Israel. Jews know who God is, and God has called the Jewish people His firstborn (see Exod. 4:23). Many Jews might not be aware of who Jesus is, but they do know who God is.

Returning to our original question, are these children and their rabbi saved for all of eternity? Who am I to say? Are they eternally lost because they did not know Jesus? Again, I will make no comment, but lay my hand on my mouth. That decision is God's business and it is safe with Him. Jews know God. They are no heathens. We sometimes forget that we were the heathens, separate from Christ, without citizenship in Israel, without the covenants of the promise, without hope and without God in the world (see Eph. 2:12). But now, we Gentiles have been permitted to come to Jesus Christ in order to know God, to pray to Him, and worship Him. We know about Him through the Word of God, the Bible, which God revealed to Israel, and of which both the Old and the New Testaments were written by Jews. I am convinced that even Luke, living in the Greek Diaspora, was a Jew, a Hellenistic Jew.

We have been saved and grafted into the root of the new covenant God made with the house of Israel and the house of Judah through Jesus Christ, our Lord, who was a Jew as well. Through Him we have come to know and adore the one and only God, the Creator of Heaven and earth, the God of Abraham, Isaac, and Jacob, the Father of our Lord Jesus Christ. But Jews by birth have it all, as Paul says in Romans 9:4-5. They are not without God, but they do have a blind spot for who Jesus is. Praise God, one day that will change as well.

God's eternal plan for His Jewish people is His business. In His anger He has sometimes acted against Israel in this world. Many perished in the desert because of their unbelief and disobedience, but does that mean that they are lost forever? That decision is not ours. Israel remains God's firstborn son, and God Himself will decide about their eternal destiny and their resurrection.

WHAT ABOUT HEATHENS?

Another question: Are heathens who have worshipped God as Creator, and whose conscience teaches them the difference between good and evil and who have tried to live accordingly, eternally lost because they do not know Jesus? Or will God judge according to what people have known of

Him? Or on the basis of what they have not known about Him? Paul writes about this in his letter to the Romans (see Rom. 2:12-16). When you do not worship God as Creator, and you are determined to go against your conscience, you will certainly be in deep trouble. Or when you as a Jew go deliberately against the Torah, then you are certainly in deep trouble. Or when you were brought up as a Christian and you deliberately turn your back on Jesus and your faith, then you are without excuse and have the worst to fear (see Rom. 1:18-32). But the final decision remains God's business (see Rom. 2:1-11; 12:17-21). Final judgment is His, and His alone.

JESUS WILL BE REVEALED TO THE JEWS

Let me share an experience of a colleague of mine. He was visiting the Great Synagogue in Jerusalem with a group of Christian Dutch tourists, when during a synagogue service, one of those present, an Orthodox Jew to all appearances, approached him and whispered, "Who are you?" (Synagogue services are different from church services in that some of those present talk in hushed tones, some pray individually, some pray together, and some pay close attention to what is happening at the front of the synagogue.) "We are a group of Dutch Christian tourists," answered my colleague, "and I am a pastor." "Then you believe that Jesus is the Messiah?" "Yes," my colleague replied. The Jewish man suddenly exclaimed, "I do too!"

Surprised, my colleague stared at him. "Yes," he said, "it became very clear to me one night" (without evangelical tracts and without anyone from a Christian mission being sent to him). "Of course, I knew what you Christians believed about Jesus, but I did not agree. However, one night it got through to me. It was revealed to me, and it simply dawned upon me that the Messiah had to be Jesus. That He really is who He said He was. And there are many more like me," he continued, "even though we are not disclosing ourselves, and we are not joining a Messianic Jewish church. We are simply staying in the synagogue. We feel quite at home here, and we speak no further about it. But we know who each of us is." Then he returned to the synagogue service.

This is a small example, a token, of what the Lord through the Holy Spirit will do for all of Israel. Jews know the Scriptures. It is their Bible. They know what we Christians believe. And when the Lord opens their eyes by the Holy Spirit, they all will see. We can leave that to the Lord, because He has promised to do so! And, of course, we can also understand our Messianic Jewish brothers and sisters who, like Paul, feel an urgency to speak to their Jewish brothers and sisters (see 1 Thess. 4:13-17; 2 Thess. 1:3-10; Phil. 3:20-21). Everyone who knows Jesus as his or her personal Savior would love to see the whole world know Him as well! Certainly, God loves us. We have a heavenly calling and are on our way to meet our heavenly Bridegroom (see Rev. 2:26-27; 19:6-10). We will one day be the Queen beside the King (see Rev. 21:1-5)!

So, the Church's task is to preach the Gospel to the ends of the earth and tell the people how good it is to know Jesus. Yet, when it comes to the Jews, we Gentiles (and we are Gentiles, no matter how much we believe in Jesus!) need to understand what a heavy load of Church history hangs around our necks. Although we desperately want, like Paul, to share our Christian faith with the Jews and share with them our hope and faith in Jesus, we should not be surprised if their reaction is similar to what we would have expected from the Dutch had the Germans returned to Holland after the Second World War to tell the Dutch that they needed to be converted. More than likely, the Dutch would have exclaimed, "Get out! Go back to your own country. Get your own house in order first!"

We Christians fail to recognize how much guilt is on our heads. Often, Jews know our Church history better than we do, and because of that, some Jews are deeply convinced that Jesus cannot be the Messiah. Undeniably, there is so much Jewish blood on the hands of His followers, the Christians, that He must be some kind of false god, lusting after Jewish blood, they think.

"But," you might ask, "does not Scripture say, '*No one comes to the Father except through Me* [Jesus]'" (John 14:6b)? Certainly, that is true. God's Word in both the Old and New Testaments is absolutely trustworthy. No one comes to the Father except through Jesus, whether one knows that or wants to admit that or not. God created the world through the Word, the Torah, who has been with Him eternally (see John 1:1-3). The Word played as a child by the Father (see Prov. 8:22-31). John says that He, Jesus, is the Word who became flesh and dwelt among us: the Torah in the flesh (see John 1:14). The world and all things that were created were made by Him (see Col. 1:15-20). God created the world through the Word, through the Torah. It all came through Him, the pre-existing Christ, and the way back to God is through Him, to the Father, whether or not you know or believe it. The Bible says so.

Jesus serves as the heavenly High Priest at the golden altar so that the prayers of the people are sanctified and cleansed before they are brought to God. No one comes to the Father but by Him. True worship is in spirit and in truth—always, in all times, and everywhere. It is a revelation of God to the heart. And everything flows from the Father through the Word and returns to Him through the same Word, which was made flesh and dwelt among us.

What a day that will be, when Israel too is allowed to see who Jesus is. And it will come! Zechariah prophesied, *"I will pour out on the house of David and the inhabitants of Jerusalem a spirit of grace and supplication. They will look on Me, the one they have pierced, and they will mourn for Him as one mourns for an only child, and grieve bitterly for Him as one grieves for a first-born son"* (Zech. 12:10; see also verses 11-14). God's firstborn son, Israel, will bitterly grieve their firstborn Son, Jesus. The whole land, all generations, men and women separately, will grieve. What a moment of recognition that will be! And who knows how soon it will come? The Lord is bringing His people back to Israel because He wants to meet them there. Israel is finally on the way to her rest, on her way to being engrafted into her own new covenant forever, and to being a blessing to the world. He will come to give Israel rest (see Jer. 31:2).

The Church has not replaced Israel; just as infant baptism has not re-placed circumcision. Israel is Israel, and the Church is the Church. God will fulfill all His promises to Israel, as He will fulfill all His promises to the Church. We need to stop mixing the two, or replacing the one with the other, as has so often happened in the past.

CHAPTER FIVE

The First "Until"—Until the Son of David Comes

*O Jerusalem, Jerusalem, you who kill the prophets and stone those sent to you, how often I have longed to gather your children together, as a hen gathers her chicks under her wings, but you were not willing. Look, your house is left to you desolate. For I tell you, you will not see Me again **until** you say, "Blessed is He who comes in the name of the Lord"* (Matthew 23:37-39).

When I was a youngster living in Holland, we celebrated Palm Sunday each year. On that day, we used unique wooden sticks with specially baked bread-chickens (or were they supposed to be roosters?) on top. In addition, there were colored ribbons, eggs, oranges, green leaves and branches; and we sang special songs—all celebrating Palm Sunday, the day that Jesus entered the city of Jerusalem, with the cheering crowds around Him.

How triumphantly Israel had cried out, *"Blessed is He who comes in the name of the Lord."* Great crowds preceded and followed Him, waving palm branches and casting their garments on the road. And as He came riding on a donkey, He fulfilled the prophecy of Zechariah, who had said, "*See, your king comes to you, righteous and having salvation, gentle and riding on a donkey, on a colt, the foal of a donkey*" (Zech 9:9b; see also Matt. 21:1-11).

Indeed, the inhabitants of Jerusalem were filled with great anticipation.

JESUS, SON OF DAVID—IN MORE WAYS THAN ONE

It is clear that everyone knew that Jesus was of the lineage of King David, because on various occasions people addressed Him as "Son of David." Even the blind beggar near Jericho called out, "*Jesus, Son of David, have mercy on me!*" (Luke 18:38b). But they probably did not realize that He was the Son of David through two lines. One was the line of His mother, Mary; the other was the line of His adoptive father, Joseph. The one line descended directly from Solomon (see Matt. 1:7), who ascended the throne after His father David, while the other line came through Nathan (see Luke 3:31), one of David's other sons (see 1 Chron. 3:5; 14:4), perhaps the eldest, who might have had a strong claim to the throne had not God's choice been otherwise (see 2 Sam. 12:24; 1 Kings 1:28-31; 2:1-4).

Solomon was the last king to rule a united Israel (see Neh. 13:26; 1 Kings 11:1-13). After him, the country was divided into two kingdoms, one containing ten tribes (Israel) and the other, two tribes (Judah). Israel lived in Samaria, and the city of Samaria was its capital. Judah was located in the area of Judea with Jerusalem as its capital. The name of Nathan, David's son, appears in the lineage of Mary, and that of Solomon in the lineage of Joseph.

But one member of Joseph's line was Coniah, of whom Jeremiah prophesied, "*...Record this man as if childless, a man who will not prosper in his lifetime, for none of his offspring will prosper, none will sit on the throne of David or rule anymore in Judah*" (Jer. 22:30). Because God's Word can be trusted, it is clear that none of Coniah's descendants would ever sit on David's throne again, even though they could trace their ancestry to Solomon. So, though the Jewish people might have considered that Jesus had a legal right to the throne of His father David, through His adoptive father, Joseph, that line had actually been blocked by the words of Jeremiah. Jesus could not have been the biological son of Joseph; if He had been, that would have blocked His access to the throne of David. But yet, through Mary, He still had access to the throne as a descendant of Nathan!

There are, of course, other reasons why Jesus could not have been a natural child of Joseph. At the beginning, at creation, had not the Lord said that from the seed of the woman the Savior would be born to crush the head of the serpent (see Gen. 3:15)? Also, did not the prophet Isaiah prophesy that a virgin would conceive and bear a son who would be called Emmanuel, God with us (see Isa. 7:14; Matt. 1:23)? It was necessary for Jesus to stand outside the line of sin of Adam, which would have come to Him through the seed of Joseph had He been a natural, biological son of Joseph. (Interesting thought, isn't it? Adam ate of the forbidden fruit, given to him by Eve, and only then did sin enter into the world. Although Eve had taken and eaten first, Paul clarifies that she was deceived by the serpent [see 2 Cor. 11:3; 1 Tim. 2:14]. It was through Adam's deed that sin entered into the world [see Rom. 5:12-19]. He apparently knew what he was doing and was held responsible.)

Anyway, Jesus had to be without sin Himself (see Rom. 5:12-14; Heb. 4:15; 9:14) in order to be the spotless Lamb who would take the sins of the world upon Himself (see John 1:19,36). Moreover, in order to sit on the throne of His father David and to rule over Jacob with a Kingdom that would have no end (see Luke 1:32-33), which is what the angel Gabriel promised to Mary, He had to be outside of Joseph's biological lineage, because of Coniah. Yet, even when the miracle of the virgin birth was unknown to His fellow Jews, He still had every legal right to the throne of His father David through His supposed father, Joseph.

THE CROWDS WILL CHEER AGAIN IN JERUSALEM

Matthew tells us that the crowd who accompanied Jesus as He rode into Jerusalem on a donkey (an animal of peace) and not on a horse (then considered an animal of war) were shouting, *"Hosanna to the son of David! Blessed is He who comes in the name of the Lord! Hosanna in the highest!"* (Matt. 21:9b). In Luke, the cry was, *"Blessed is the king who comes in the name of the Lord!"*

(Luke 19:38a). Luke also reports that *"As He approached Jerusalem and saw the city, He wept over it and said, 'If you, even you, had only known on this day what would bring you peace—but now it is hidden from your eyes'"* (Luke 19:41-42). And when something is hidden, one simply cannot see it.

Jesus looked far past the cheering crowd surrounding Him and declared,

> *The days will come upon you when your enemies will build an embankment against you and encircle you and hem you in on every side. They will dash you to the ground, you and the children within your walls* ["*His blood be on us, and on our children*" (Matt. 27:25b; see also Acts 5:28)]. *They will not leave one stone on another, because you did not recognize the time of God's coming to you* (Luke 19:43-44).

Jesus knew that this entrance into Jerusalem was the way to the cross, not the way to the throne of His father David. He knew that He would freely give His life (see John 10:17-18), so that as the Prince of Peace He would establish true peace between God and men by removing the stumbling block of sin. He knew this had to happen first, before He could usher in the Kingdom. And He also knew that one day in the future the crowds in Jerusalem would once again shout, *"Blessed is He who comes in the name of the Lord."*

In His mind's eye, He saw first the cross, then the resurrection and the ascension, then the terrible fall of the city of Jerusalem and the destruction of the temple in A.D. 70 by the Roman legions. Then He saw nearly two thousand years later, when the Jews would be scattered all over the world, and then...the city of Jerusalem again, a Jewish State once more, and another triumphant entry, when yet again there would be the shout, *"Blessed is He who comes in the name of the Lord."*

He had said, *"You shall not see Me again...."* But He did not say, "From now on you shall never see Me again." Indeed, Israel will not see Him again until they greet Him as the great Son of David who shall ascend the throne of His father David in Jerusalem: *"Blessed is He who comes in the name of the Lord"* (Matt. 23:39b). One day He shall reign in the midst of Jacob, just as the angel Gabriel had announced.

This will not be a spiritual, heavenly reign. After His ascension, He did not approach David in Heaven and say, "With all respect, father David, I need to sit now on your throne here in Heaven to reign over Jacob, so please move over." No. David's throne stood in Jerusalem. Since His ascension, Jesus has had all power/authority in Heaven and on earth, and He sits with His Father, the eternal God, on His throne (see Matt. 28:18-20; Rev. 3:21; 4:2-3; 5:6-7). But when He returns, He will sit on the throne of His father David in Jerusalem (see Ps. 89:27- 29,36-37; 2 Sam. 7:12-16).

There will be a short period of darkness all over the world, and then that time will arrive. The stage is presently being set in the Middle East with a reestablished Jerusalem in a reestablished Israel and a reestablished Jewish people, surrounded by a new "Roman" empire and all the Old Testament enemies in the Arab countries. The miracle of the national rebirth of these enemies is as great as that of Israel. Jesus had said, "*Look at the fig tree and all the trees*" (Luke 21:29b). The whole forest is back in place in the form of Israel and its surrounding hostile countries. We are awaiting the arrival of the main Actor on the world stage who will bring this terrible phase of world history to a happy ending—happy for Israel as He comes to give her rest, and happy for us who will rest along with Israel, although in a different way.

Isn't it remarkable that Jesus came from Bethany on the Mount of Olives (see Matt. 21:2) to the city and that Zechariah saw Him returning to the Mount of Olives (see Zech. 14:3-4) and from there entering the city? Ezekiel, too, saw God's glory returning to the temple, entering from the east (see Ezek. 10; 11:22-23; 43:1-7).

THE ABOMINATION OF DESOLATION

After Jesus had uttered His prophecies about the future of Jerusalem, He left the temple. It says, significantly (see Matt. 24:1), that He would not be returning to it, for everything that the temple represents was present in Him, in His body. And that temple was to be destroyed and…rebuilt in three days! (see John 2:13-22; Matt. 26:61; 27:40; Mark 14:58; 15:29).

On the third day, He would rise from the dead.

Jesus loved the temple in Jerusalem, so much so that in great anger He confronted the commercial traffic and business that religion had caused, Even then, the temple had become more of a money-making machine than a place of worship. With a whip He drove everything and everyone—sheep, cattle, and moneychangers—out of the temple. While He overturned the tables of the moneychangers, scattering their coins on the ground, He was somewhat gentler with the sellers of doves (the offerings of the poor), ordering them to take their wares and leave (see John 2:14-16). The zeal for God's house had consumed Him (see John 2:17; Ps. 69:9). Whenever He and His disciples had been in Jerusalem, they could be found daily in the temple (see Matt. 26:55; Luke 21:37; 22:53). As a boy, a "son of the law" like every other Jewish boy of His age, He had had His bar-mitzvah there, and afterwards He had stayed behind in the temple, where He wanted to be about His Father's business (see Luke 2:40-52).

Now, with His disciples, He left His beloved temple and went to the Mount of Olives, with its wonderful view of the whole city and especially of the beautiful buildings of the temple. When the disciples proudly pointed out the temple complex that Herod had magnificently restored, Jesus said to them, *"I tell you the truth, not one stone here will be left on another; every one will be thrown down"* (Matt. 24:2b). This prophecy was fulfilled with horrible accuracy by the Romans 40 years later, in A.D. 70.

Luke records that Jesus said:

> *When you see Jerusalem being surrounded by armies, you will know that its desolation is near. Then let those who are in Judea flee to the mountains, let those in the city get out, and let those in the country not enter the city. For this is the time of punishment in fulfillment of all that has been written. How dreadful it will be in those days for pregnant women and nursing mothers [because they cannot flee quickly]! There will be great distress in the land and wrath against this people. They will fall by the sword and will be taken as prisoners to all the nations* (Luke 21:20-24a).

After the uprising under Bar Kochba in A.D. 135, Jerusalem was again taken by the Romans, razed to the ground, and reestablished as a Roman city, Aelia Capitolina, with entry forbidden to Jews. *"Jerusalem will be trampled on by the Gentiles **until** [the second "until," but more about that in the next chapter] the times of the Gentiles are fulfilled"* (Luke 21:24b). *"Look, your house is left to you desolate,"* He had said, *"until you say, 'Blessed is He who comes in the name of the Lord'"* (Matthew 23:38,39b).

Even before His death and resurrection (it was still two days before Passover, when He would be handed over to be crucified—see Matt. 26:1-2), while sitting on the Mount of Olives, Jesus prophesied His return. After centuries of "signs" (compare, for example, Matthew 24:3-14 with Revelation 6), He saw Jerusalem surrounded again. He foresaw the "abomination of desolation," standing in the holy place (a rebuilt temple, or the two mosques that are standing there right now?), as prophesied by Daniel the prophet. And again, He advised the Jews in that future to flee. *"Pray that your flight will not take place in winter* [on account of bad weather] *or on the Sabbath* [because all traffic in Israel is at a standstill]. *For then there will be great distress, unequaled from the beginning of the world until now—and never to be equaled again"* (Matt. 24:20-21; see also verses 15-19).

These things were not totally fulfilled when Jerusalem was captured by the Roman Legions in A.D. 70. There was no "abomination of desolation" in the temple then, and no defilement comparable with that of Antiochus Epiphanes in 167 B.C. when this Hellenistic ruler forbade the Jews to practice circumcision or keep the Sabbath. This Greek-Syrian usurper placed a statue of the Greek god Zeus (Jupiter) in the temple and offered sacrifices of swine (the most unclean animal of all animals for Jews, according to the law of Moses). His actions led directly to the Maccabean revolt, and Jewish victory! After that, the Jews cleansed the temple and purified it in order to restore the service to the one true God. Still today, the Jews celebrate Chanukah to remember this victory and the rededication of the temple.

Jesus foresaw a similar kind of abomination in the endtimes, when Jerusalem would again be a city and the capital of a Jewish State of Israel.

WHEN WILL HE COME?

People have always asked this question. Nobody knows the answer, not even the angels, not even the Son (see Matt. 24:36). Only the Father knows the moment when He will say to His Son, "Now You must return to earth to fulfill all the promises I have made about the Kingdom that would come." Hence, we must be prepared every day. Never trust anyone who answers with all kinds of calculations or impressive schemes or schedules as if he has been consulting a train timetable. The Bible is not a jigsaw puzzle of which people can debate how the pieces should fit together. If the Lord would have wanted us to know the order of events, He would have provided that information in the Scriptures. But He did not. The only order of events that I know of in the Bible is found in Matthew chapter 24, the great discourse of Jesus Himself about the future.

Even the disciples, sitting on the Mount of Olives, asked Jesus when He would return, but Jesus did not give them a direct answer. What He did say to them (and to us) is, *"Watch out that no one deceives you"* (Matt. 24:4). First, there will be false christs, false prophets, wars, famines, hatred, lawlessness, plagues, earthquakes, a lack of love, the fall of Jerusalem, and a worldwide dispersion of the Jews.

But there will be also two positive signs: the preaching of the Gospel of the Kingdom to the whole world, as a testimony to all nations (that is, to the whole non-Jewish, Gentile world—see Matt. 24:14); and there will be the return of the Jews to the land of Israel, the restoration of the fig tree with new leaves and new life (see Luke 21:29-31). Then the Kingdom of God is near. Then the end will come. Jerusalem will be on the world scene again, and there will be an "abomination of desolation" in the holy place and such oppression as has never been seen before. But for the sake of the elect, those days will be shortened; otherwise, no one would survive.

ARE YOU READY FOR HIS COMING?

The signs of the times indicate that His coming is rapidly approaching; the Jews are being reestablished in their own land; and Jerusalem and many other ruined cities in Israel are being rebuilt. But He might come for you at any time that He gives orders to His angels to bring you to Him. At any moment, He may take you to Himself. Then you will see Him, just as He is (see 1 John 3:2)! Whoever worships Him now, who kneels before His cross, and receives Him as his or her personal Savior and Lord, and confesses all sins, will receive cleansing through His shed blood and will know, "I too belong to Him. He is my Lord and Savior! Heaven is my home! And when He comes, I will be forever with Him and I will participate in His future that will last for all eternity."

CHAPTER SIX

The Second "Until"—Until the Times of the Gentiles Are Fulfilled

*There will be great distress in the land and wrath against this people. They will fall by the sword and will be taken as prisoners to all the nations. Jerusalem will be trampled on by the Gentiles **until** the times of the Gentiles are fulfilled (Luke 21:23b-24).*

All four written Gospels—Matthew, Mark, Luke, and John—are needed to give us a complete picture. However, although they certainly complement one another and are not contradictory, it can be difficult sometimes to determine the exact chronological order of events when reading them. I encourage you to prayerfully consider the seeming inconsistencies, and the Lord will lead you into a revelation of more truth. That has been my experience in the past 35 years of my life as a Christian, despite all the arguments of "higher criticism."

Matthew's record of the words of Jesus regarding the latter days looks into the far distant future. He sees a rebuilt Jerusalem, an "abomination" in the holy place, and great distress such as has never been or ever will be again (see Matt. 24:15-22); whereas, Luke's account puts more emphasis on Jesus' words about the near future, a fulfillment in the days that lie directly ahead. Here, Jesus spoke of the imminent fall of Jerusalem and the worldwide scattering of the Jewish people among the Gentile (the non-Jewish) people of the world—the "Roman" exile. Today, we can see the record of these events in the pictures on the triumphal Arch of Titus in Rome. Titus was the general who conquered Jerusalem and destroyed the city and the temple. Pictures of Jewish prisoners have been chiseled into the stone arch, as well as pictures of the stolen treasures from the temple, including the golden menorah with its seven branches. Countless Jews were killed or sold as slaves. Indeed, the slave market was so flooded with Jewish slaves that the price of slaves dropped dramatically.

However, in Matthew, Jesus spoke of another time, claiming that Jerusalem would be trampled underfoot by the Gentiles, until the times of the Gentiles were fulfilled. When will those times be fulfilled? When Jesus returns in glory!

The title of the Book of Revelation means "unveiling," as when a statue is officially unveiled for all to see. Accordingly, the Book of Revelation unveils Jesus Christ, showing us the public appearance of His coming in glory, as well as how Jerusalem will be trampled on by the Gentiles up to and including the very last and greatest oppression or tribulation (see Rev. 11:1-2). Only when Jesus Himself appears will the Gentiles be shattered and broken like pottery with His rod of iron (see Rev. 19:11-16; Ps. 2:9). Only when His feet again stand on the Mount of Olives, from where He ascended to Heaven (see Acts 1:9-11), will the warring nations that have come up against Jerusalem be defeated.

Then the city will no longer be trampled underfoot by the Gentiles (see Zech. 12:2-3; 14:2-7; Joel 3:12-17). We are on our way to that glorious moment. The times of the Gentiles are coming to an end.

JERUSALEM CONTINUES TO BE TRAMPLED

But according to some, the times of the Gentiles have already ended. "Look," they say, "at the reestablishment of the Jewish State in 1948." In spite of all the problems, Israel was able to celebrate its 50th anniversary in 1998, the first Year of Jubilee (see Lev. 25; 27) since the establishment of the state, even though the actual religious Year of Jubilee was a few years later. And Israel will undoubtedly be able to celebrate its 60th anniversary in 2008. In 2007, they also celebrated the 40th anniversary of the reunification of the city of Jerusalem. "Surely," some say, "the times of the Gentiles ended in 1967, when the city of Jerusalem was reunited and became the undivided capital of the State of Israel."

In that year, Israel freed East Jerusalem from the Jordanian occupation that this part of the city had suffered since the proclamation of the Jewish State in 1948. In those 19 years, a mere blip in Jerusalem's three-thousand-year history, countless synagogues in East Jerusalem had been demolished or turned into public latrines, and it was the only time that the city had ever been divided; thus, any Palestinian claim to a part of the city is historically invalid. Then Israel declared Jerusalem the undivided capital of the independent State of Israel. Those who argue that the end of the times of the Gentiles occurred in 1967 point to this event. "See for yourself," they say. "Jerusalem is no longer under the feet of Gentiles."

But is that really the case? Are there no Gentiles ruling in Jerusalem? What about the fact that Europe and the United Nations are telling Israel what to do with their own land and their own city, Jerusalem? Moreover, the Arab world controls the most holy place in Jerusalem—the Temple Mount.

The Scriptures also seem to indicate that the times of the Gentiles have not yet been fulfilled, for they declare that these times will come to an end with the coming of the Messiah, the return of Christ. We must not lose sight of the important fact that the holiest place in Jerusalem, in the heart of the city, is still closed to the Jews. Gentiles rule there. The Temple Mount is governed by the Islamic world. It is still *für Juden verboten* (forbidden to Jews).

At one time, the temple stood in this place. There, on Mount Moriah, which is Mount Zion, Abraham was prepared to sacrifice Isaac (see Gen. 22:1-19). His faith and trust in the Lord were such that he believed God was able to bring his son back from the dead, and in a sense, this was so (see Heb. 11:17-19). God chose this place as a dwelling place for His name (see Deut. 12:11). He guided David to choose the exact spot (see 1 Chron. 21:21–22:1), and his son Solomon built the temple there (see 1 Kings 5:5). After the Babylonian captivity, the temple that had been destroyed by King Nebuchadnezzar was rebuilt under the leadership of Ezra and Nehemiah. It was much smaller than Solomon's temple, and the elderly who remembered the original temple wept at its dedication (see Ezra 3:12). The second temple, greatly enlarged and embellished by King Herod (the same Herod who had murdered the children of Bethlehem) was destroyed by Titus in A.D. 70.

Today it is the site of two Islamic shrines, or mosques. So this place is still trampled under foot by Gentiles (i.e., non-Jews). Arabs continue to wave the scepter there.

THE SPREAD OF ISLAM BY FIRE AND SWORD

Of course, there are many Muslims who, because of their upbringing, honestly believe that Allah is the one and only true God and accordingly try to serve him with their whole heart. Indeed, there are millions of peace-loving Muslim people around the world. However, a tree will always be known by its fruits, with regard to every human being, including Christians, Jews, Muslims, and people of other religions, or even of non-religious thinking. In Christian as well as in Muslim religion, there have always been extremist lines of teaching that have led to hatred and bloodshed. But when you really know and serve the one and only God, there is love in your heart, not hatred, because God is love.

An elderly Jewish lady once told me, "I don't care under what circumstances or in what religion you were born. You could not help that. It was not your choice. Whether you were born in a Hindu family, or a Muslim one, or a Jewish one, or a Christian one, or raised in the Confucianism of China, or in the Shintoism of Japan, or in whatever religion or non-religious lines of thinking and believing—you were not asked whether you approved or not. But the moment you became a certain age, started to think for yourself, and were able to make your decisions about your faith and your lifestyle, then you were responsible yourself. So if you want to be sure whether the God you are serving is the one and only true God, you can verify that. Because when you know and serve the one and only true God, there will be love in your heart, not hatred, because God is love. You will love God and your fellow human beings as yourself."

Christians should understand God's love. Then, when you read the hate preached by the church fathers, by the medieval church, by Luther and others, your heart should become chilled, because you realize that this cannot be from God; this cannot be from Jesus Christ, but must come from evil sources, cloaked in Christian garments. Every human being should look deep into his own heart to see what the fruit of the spirit is of the God he or she is serving—love or hatred.

Historically, Islam has spread by fire and by sword. Twice, Christian Europe was nearly overrun. The first time occurred in the Middle Ages when the Islamic advance was halted in the Pyrenees, the mountains between France and Spain, by the Christian knights of Charles Martel, the grandfather of Charlemagne—A.D. 732 at Tours. The second time was in the 17th century, when an Islamic army reached the gates of Vienna, A.D. 1683. Today, for the time being, Islam spreads by peaceful immigration of Islamic workers who benefit the economy of Europe and other parts of the world. As a minority, they obey the laws of the country in which they live. However, as soon as they become a majority, things will rapidly change. Then, often Muslim-law, sharia-law, starts to set in.

I will never forget a personal experience I had about 25 years ago. In those days, I was a producer of radio and television programs at a Dutch Christian network. We had produced a documentary about the genocide that the Muslim Turks afflicted on the Christian Armenians between 1895 and 1918. The Armenians are the oldest nation on earth who officially adopted Christianity as their religion in A.D. 301. By the hands of the Muslim Turks, between 1.5 and 2.5 million Armenians were slaughtered, many of them even literally crucified.

On the day that the program was to be aired, 2000 Turks demonstrated in front of our office building in Holland, and I received threatening letters from various Islamic individuals and organizations. They told me, "Yes, you can now still say what you like, but the day is rapidly coming that we will tell you what to say or to be silent about. And we are on the winning side. Look how many Christian churches are closed or turned into mosques and how many new mosques are opened."

Then I understood for the first time that some of these workers from foreign Islamic countries understand themselves as not only a benefit to our economies, not just present to earn some money or to flee some terrible situation in their home countries, but to be available to conquer the world for Allah. One day the whole world will be under Allah, Mohammed has promised them. Needless to say, we did broadcast the documentary; however, my family and I needed personal police protection for some time.

For Muslims, conquest of the world is a promise and a duty rooted in the Koran revealed to Mohammed between A.D. 589 and A.D. 632, a holy book that shares stories with Judeo-Christian texts, "translated" into a Muslim context. In 711–718, the Arabs conquered Spain, which became a center of commerce and Islamic culture. In 1453, the Ottoman Turks took Constantinople, capital of Orthodox Christianity. In 1492, King Ferdinand drove the Moors from Spain and then expelled the Jews. In 1683, the Ottoman siege of Vienna failed, marking the end of Islamic expansion.

The concept of a *jihad*, or holy war, is an official doctrine of the Islamic faith. Whereas, to spread the Christian faith by the sword is not in the Bible! It is a distortion of the teachings of Jesus! According to the Koran, however, anyone dying while engaged in a *jihad* goes straight to paradise. Others can never be sure of their fate, and can only hope that things will work out in the end and that Allah will accept them. Consequently, Muslims must commit themselves totally to the religious duties prescribed by Islam.

The five most important of these duties are:

1. To say the *salat*, the required prayers, five times a day, facing the holy city of Mecca.

2. To pay the *zakat*, the church tax.

3. To give alms to the poor.

4. To celebrate Ramadan, in which one fasts during the day for 30 days and can only eat and drink after sunset.

5. To perform the *hajj*, the pilgrimage to Mecca, at least once in a lifetime, but preferably more often.

These are the five pillars of Islam; and the *jihad*, the holy war, some say, could be considered the sixth pillar.

Meanwhile, Islam reigns in the heart of Jerusalem; it dominates the Temple Mount. Hatred for Jews and Christians is promoted there. Some say there is no need to wait for any further "abomination of desolation" in the holy place. It has already been present on Mount Zion for centuries.

PERSECUTION BY CHRISTIANS

Some will respond to the comments in the previous section, regarding the violent acts of Islam, by pointing out that what has been done under the banner of the cross in history also beggars description. Think about the behavior of the "Christian" knights during the medieval crusades, as they wrested the holy places from Islam and ruled over the Holy Land for two hundred years. When they conquered the city of Jerusalem, they drove the Jews who lived there—men, women, children, and old people—into the Great Synagogue and set fire to it, burning them alive; and the next day they celebrated Holy Communion.

It is also true that after A.D. 650, the Jews were better off under Islam than they were in the lands of Christendom for the next 1300 years. Even though Jews in the Islamic world were from time to time robbed of money and goods, they were seldom put to death, and in general, they were able to practice their religion and culture. By contrast, in the lands of Christendom, where the Christian message was that the Jews were the murderers of Jesus, people saw to it that the Jews were persecuted, robbed, and murdered, and their religious books burned.

In addition, Jews living along the Rhine were murdered and robbed in order to finance the medieval crusades. The Nazi did not come up with the idea of making Jews wear the Star of David during the Second World War on their own; the practice actually dates back to the Middle Ages when the church made Jews wear distinctive clothes, such as a round patch of cloth or a special Jewish hat. During the Roman Catholic Inquisition in the southern lands of Europe, thousands of Jews who refused to convert to Christianity were burned at the stake, with crucifixes held before their eyes. The 19th and 20th-century pogroms in the Christian countries of Eastern Europe were often encouraged and launched by Russian Orthodox priests and clergymen, especially around the time of Easter when they would call upon the people "to teach the Jews, the 'God-killers,' a lesson."

The Holocaust took place in Lutheran Germany, and apparently there were not enough people opposed to what happened to the Jews to prevent the terrible deaths of six million Jews (including one and a half million children) in the concentration camps; although individual Christians, both Protestant and Roman Catholic, in countries such as the Netherlands, Germany, Poland, and Denmark, did risk their own lives to do what they could to help the Jews. But we all know—and the Jews know—that the Pope in Rome (who is considered by Jews to be the leader of Christianity) was silent. And it is well-known that war criminals were harbored in some Catholic monasteries after the war (although it should not be forgotten that during the war many Jews in Italy were sheltered in some Roman Catholic monasteries). We know of the conduct of some German Christians who collaborated with the Nazi regime, although individuals like Dietrich Bonhoeffer gave their lives in an attempt to resist it.

Throughout history, many barbaric deeds have been done in the name of Christianity under the "banner of the cross," including the colonization of the world and the killing of natives in order to rob them of their gold and other precious metals and natural resources. Even the Bible was quoted and used in defense of slavery.

So to be fair in the presentation of the depth of the conflict between Jews, Christians, and Muslims, one must be open and honest to all sides and present the facts as they are and historically have been over the centuries. To ignore them or present them in a one-sided way does not help to provide real solutions to real problems.

Anyone who knows the Bible, knows that such terrible behavior has absolutely nothing to do with Jesus Christ. These actions cannot be deduced from the teachings of the New Testament, but are a terrible travesty of them. The Christian faith does not uphold the concept of "a holy war." The *Gott mit uns* (God with us) written on the belts of German soldiers had more to do with taking God's name in vain than with praying. Christendom has so much guilt of its own that it has little right to point the finger at others. Moreover, Christendom has very little to do with the true Christian faith that lives out the atonement of Christ, which speaks of forgiveness and of a loving God, even as He loves us, and of loving our neighbor as ourselves.

SPIRITUAL CONFLICT

Judaism began with Abraham, about 2000 years before Christ; Christianity began with Jesus, at the beginning of the Christian calendar; and Islam began with Mohammed, about 600 years after Christ. While Islam acknowledges links to Judaism and Christianity, it regards itself as entrusted with the last and definitive revelation of God, Allah. It is inconceivable to Muslims that the Holy Places in Israel should be in the hands of religions that were mere way stations on the path to Islam. Jerusalem is the Muslims' third holy city (after Mecca and Medina). It is held to be holy (even though it is never mentioned in the Koran) because one night in a dream Mohammed reportedly ascended on his horse to heaven from Jerusalem. The print of the hoof of that horse is still pointed out in the Mosque of Omar on the Temple Mount! In the Koran, a place is mentioned as the most distant mosque/holy place—Al Quds—without telling where that place is located.

In the days of Mohammed, there was neither a mosque nor a temple in Jerusalem; some historians believe the Koran is referring to the opposite direction from Mecca, to the village of Janad in Yemen, where in A.D. 615 the Al-Janadiya-Mosque was built, the most distant mosque/holy place. These scholars believe that it was from here that Mohammed made his trip to heaven. But today, for whatever reason, Muslims point to Jerusalem as the holy place the Koran is referring to, although when Muslims in Israel pray, they turn their backs on Jerusalem and pray towards the direction of Mecca.

Muslims insist that Jerusalem be returned to them and their rule. Because Israel was under Allah for over 1000 years and Allah is all-powerful, it simply cannot be that this small piece of land—Israel—and the third holy city of Islam—Jerusalem—would ever go back to religions that are considered by Islam to be stations-passed-by, like Judaism and Christianity. They consider themselves to have the one and only true religion; and to permit these sacred Muslim sites to remain in the hands of others, whether Jewish or Christian, gives the impression that those religions and their God are stronger than Allah. And that is out of the question.

Today many underestimate the role of Islam in the conflict in the Middle East. This conflict is not primarily about oil, or about a homeland for displaced Palestinians, or about any political or economic interests. It is, on the deepest level, a religious conflict, between the God of Abraham, Isaac, and Jacob, the Father of our Lord Jesus Christ, and all other gods, powers, ideologies, and religions of the world.

Christians—and Jews—do not have holy places, but have a holy God, whom they wish to serve with holy lives. Still, some places do have symbolic value for their faith as well. And the fact remains that the holiest site in Jerusalem, the site of the temple, is in non-Jewish, Gentile hands, and that Jews cannot even access it for prayer. They must stay below, at the foot of the remains of the huge walls built by Herod, which once surrounded the temple complex. They pray at the Western Wall (the Wailing Wall), which is a remnant of the second temple, built after the Babylonian captivity under Ezra and Nehemiah and enlarged by Herod. That is as close as they can get to the place where the holy of holies was located in the temple without running the risk of stepping unaware upon that most holy spot.

So instead of speaking about the "three monotheistic religions"—Judaism, Christianity, and Islam, some say we should realize the fact that there is only one monotheistic religion—Judaism. And that Christianity is a branch growing upon that old root. And that Islam is another religion, albeit monotheistic.

ISHMAEL OR ISRAEL

When one looks at the heartbreaking conflict in the Middle East, one cannot help but think about the biblical background. And perhaps we can find some solutions and understanding there. What has the Bible to say about the conflict between these two brothers with the same father, Abraham, but with different mothers? Ishmael, who is considered to be the forefather of the Arab nations, was born to his Egyptian mother, Hagar, who was a maidservant to Abraham's wife, Sarah; and Isaac was born to Abraham's wife, Sarah, and is the forefather of the Jewish people, of Israel. From a biblical perspective, let's consider the positions and rights that each of these half brothers were granted.

When Abraham was 99 years of age and Sarah was past the age of childbearing, the Lord God visited Abraham, and told him that his wife, Sarah, would have a baby of her own.

We read in Genesis 17:17-22:

> *Abraham fell facedown; he laughed and said to himself, "Will a son be born to a man a hundred years old? Will Sarah bear a child at the age of ninety?" And Abraham said to God, "If only Ishmael might live under Your blessing!" Then God said, "Yes, but your wife Sarah will bear you a son, and you will call him Isaac. I will establish My covenant with him as an everlasting covenant for his descendants after him. And as for Ishmael, I have heard you: I will surely bless him; I will make him fruitful and will greatly increase his numbers. He will be the father of twelve rulers, and I will make him into a*

great nation. But My covenant I will establish with Isaac, whom Sarah will bear to you by this time next year." When He had finished speaking with Abraham, God went up from him.

As we read in this Scripture, Ishmael, the Arab nations, have the promise of the blessing of God. He has promised them that they would be fruitful and would be a great nation. Today, there are between 200 and 300 million Arabs, living in over 20 different and independent nations in the Middle East, in a vast area of very oil-rich land. They are powerful enough to choke the world's economy if they would prefer to do so. Indeed, the existence of these mighty and powerful nations prove that God has kept His promise and has blessed Ishmael tremendously.

And Israel? After all the slaughters throughout the centuries, there remain only about 15 million Jews in the world. In Israel (a country smaller than tiny Holland, which you can hardly find on a world map!) live about five to six million Jews, in a land with no oil. Another four to five million live in the USA, about one to two million in the former Soviet Union, and the rest still scattered around the globe. A Jewish friend told me, "It is not fun to be the chosen people of God. I wish He would have chosen someone else! It would have been better for us to have God's blessings than His covenant, because that means a lot of suffering."

Indeed, the prophet Zechariah prophesied about Israel in Zechariah 13:8, *"'In the whole earth,' declares the Lord, 'two-thirds* [of Israel] *will be struck down and perish; yet one-third will be left in it.'"* (*Earth* is the correct translation, instead of *"in the whole land"*; compare with Zechariah 14:9—*"the Lord will be King over the whole earth."*) And when one adds up all the numbers of Jews who have been massacred throughout the ages, the statistics reveal that in history, two thirds of the Jewish people have been wiped out, and only one third is left. Even if one translates Zechariah 13:8 as "in the whole land," meaning "Eretz Israel," the "land of Israel," this prophecy has been fulfilled as well. At the hands of the Romans in A.D. 70 and A.D. 135, over two million Jews were slaughtered, and the rest, almost totally, were led into captivity?although there have always been Jews living in Israel, also during the last 2000 years!

When we add the numbers of the killing of the Jews over the centuries—with the final slaughter of six million under the Nazi regime in Germany—the conclusion can be drawn that over the ages, two thirds of the Jews have been wiped out, and only one third is left.

So to think that in the near future, Israel will become "one big Auschwitz" during the "time of Jacob's trouble," the "tribulation," is not necessarily according to Scriptures, although difficult times for Israel are still to come. In Jeremiah 30:7 and Daniel 12:1, we read that Israel will be saved in these terrible times, not destroyed—cleansed, but not wiped out. Yes, the remaining one third will be cleansed by fire, but not destroyed—cleansed in order that the pure gold will remain (see Zech. 13:7-9).

The process of redemption has started, not the process of annihilation. The order of events listed in Zechariah 13:7-9 describes the history of the Jewish people in a nutshell. First, the Shepherd Jesus is killed. Then the people of Israel are scattered. Then two thirds perish, even the little ones—1.5 million children were murdered in Auschwitz. Then the remaining one third in the land will be purified so that in the end: *They will call on My Name and I will answer them; I will say, 'They are My people,' and they will say, 'The Lord is our God'"* (Zech. 13:9b).

There are blessings for Ishmael, but God's everlasting covenant was made with Abraham, and later confirmed to Isaac, and later to Jacob. The Bible says that all the peoples and the nations of the earth must bless Israel…and then they will be blessed by God. But when they curse Israel, they will be cursed, according to Genesis 12:1-3. The issue is not determining who "Ishmael" is, for we know there are great blessings for "Ishmael." The issue is whether or not one respects God's promises and covenants with Israel and the Jewish people. We, the "Christian world," and every other nation, including the "Islamic" world, must learn this lesson. If we do, we will be blessed.

WORLD POWERS

When did "the times of the Gentiles" begin? Some say it was when Solomon's temple was destroyed by the Babylonians under Nebuchadnezzar in 586 B.C.. Since that time, Israel has never been totally independent. One kingdom after another has overrun it. Of course, there was the smaller, second temple built in Jerusalem when a remnant of the Jews returned from the Babylonian exile, but Israel remained a part or a province of a much larger empire. Sometimes it enjoyed limited autonomy, and it was even moderately independent at times; but never again was it as powerful and independent as in the days of David and Solomon.

During the days of Daniel the prophet, Daniel served at the court of the Babylonian king, Nebuchadnezzar. In the second year of Nebuchadnezzar's reign, Daniel was able to tell the king what the king had seen in his dream and interpret the dream for him, because the God of Heaven had revealed the mystery to Daniel.

The king had dreamed of a statue with a head of gold, breast and arms of silver, belly and thighs of bronze, legs of iron, and feet that were partly of iron and partly of clay. He saw a stone roll down and strike the statue, pulverizing it. The stone then grew into a great mountain that filled the whole earth (see Dan. 2). Daniel explained that the different parts of the statue represented four or five successive kingdoms (the last kingdom being in a sense an extension or continuation of the fourth one). The golden head was interpreted as the Babylonian kingdom; the silver breast and arms as the empire of the Medes and Persians; and the belly and thighs of bronze represented the Greek Empire under Alexander the Great. The legs of iron represented the Roman Empire, which divided into the Eastern and Western Empires, the feet of iron and clay. The fifth and last kingdom appeared to be a revival of the Roman Empire on a worldwide scale.

In subsequent visions, more details were revealed to Daniel. Babylon, the golden head, was represented by a winged lion. The Medes and the Persians (the silver breast and arms) were seen as a bear with three ribs in its mouth (possibly representing Syria, Babylon, and Egypt, which it "devoured"). The Greek–Macedonian kingdom (the bronze belly) was seen as a leopard with four wings and four heads, representing the fact that after the death of Alexander, his empire was divided into four kingdoms—Egypt, Syria, Macedonia, and Asia Minor—ruled by four of his generals. The fourth kingdom, the Roman Empire (the iron legs and feet) was seen as a monstrous beast with ten horns, from which a small horn emerges that takes over the whole earth (see Dan. 7).

The coming of the Son of Man marks the end of the last kingdom and the establishment of the eternal Kingdom of the Son of Man. Because His coming will destroy the whole statue at once, it seems that in the endtimes, the whole statue, that is, all of the empires that it represents, will be revived and present on the world scene in some way or another (see Dan. 2:31-35). The same beasts, which Daniel saw, reappear in the Book of Revelation (see Rev. 13).

Between the fall of the Roman Empire and the arrival of that last kingdom, there have been numerous conquerors of the Promised Land, including the Byzantines, Persians, Arabs, Crusaders, Mamelukes, Turks, French, and British. Indeed, many Gentile feet have trampled upon Jerusalem and the Holy Land. Furthermore, the European Union is in some sense a revived Roman empire (although this time it is part of a world in which there are more and larger power blocks than existed in the time of the writers of the Bible). Communism has collapsed in Russia (allowing the Jews there to return home—see Jer. 16:14-15), and more and more the map of Europe appears as it did under the Romans. The United Nations, a kind of world parliament, though sometimes powerless, is gaining influence, and the blue helmets of its peacekeepers are seen more often everywhere in the world. Increasing economic developments, the energy and environmental crises, and the conflicts erupting all over the world demand a global response. The arrival of the last world kingdom is fast approaching. World peace appears to be within our grasp, facilitated by computer and satellite systems, cable communication and mass media, and multinational, financial institutions and investments. The global village is becoming a reality. But let us beware of shouting, "Peace, peace" where there is no peace, and keep alert!

"Until" Promises the End of Persecution and the Beginning of an Eternal Kingdom

There can be no permanent peace yet, for the Bible assures us that the antichrist still has to appear. He will be a pseudo-Christ in the place of (and opposed to) the real Christ. The Greek word *anti* can mean both "against" and "in the place of, instead of." When he appears, the Gentiles will again tread Jerusalem underfoot, literally, until the times of the Gentiles are ful- filled. The whole world will be part of the system set up by the antichrist, and anyone opposing that system will not be able to buy or sell. They will be marginalized, persecuted, imprisoned, and even killed (see Rev. 13:11-18), just as Christians were persecuted during the Nazi regime and under com- munist dictatorships, and still are in the contemporary Islamic world.

When that happens, we will come to appreciate the significance of the little word "until" in Luke 21:24! It promises that the persecution of those days soon will end. That terrible situation will not endure forever. The Gen- tiles will not have the final word. Oppression, persecution, murder, cruelty, hunger, sickness, and death will not have the final say in this world. Christ will have the last word, when He destroys the powers of darkness and kills the lawless one, the antichrist, and sets up His own Kingdom. Ultimately, He is Israel's only hope. He is the Church's only hope. He is the world's only hope. You may be armed to the teeth, as Israel is today, but you will be pow- erless against the whole world unless, as when David faced Goliath, God is on your side and gives you the victory (see 1 Sam. 17:47).

How encouraged the people in Holland would have been had they known in advance that the Second World War and the Nazi regime would last for only five years. But they did not know that, and some must have feared that the regime would last forever. This fear led to a loss of hope and faith, and an end to resistance. For our encouragement, the Bible assures us that the antichrist's final worldwide reign will be limited in length, lasting for a mere three and a half years, 1260 days (a time + 2 times + half a time = 3 and a half times = 42 months). What a relief! The mere existence of Israel it- self and the return of the Jewish people as a fulfillment of biblical prophecy is a sign of hope. God is still in charge and leading history toward His final goal, the establishment of His eternal Kingdom. He will come to give Israel rest.

All of Israel will be saved (see Rom. 11:26), the law will go forth from Jerusalem (see Isa. 2:2-4; Zech. 12:10-14), and the nations will no longer learn war (see Mic. 4:1-3). The power of Allah and Islam will be broken, for God loves the Arabs and the Palestinians. Ishmael, Abraham's other son besides Isaac, the progenitor of the Arabs, has received great promises from God (see Gen. 21:18; 17:20-22). Jesus wants to set them free too.

The Bible says that a highway will be built from Egypt to Assyria (today's Iraq), and that Assyrians will go to Egypt and Egyptians to Assyria, and both will worship God together. They will worship not Allah, but YHWH, the God of Abraham, Isaac, and Jacob, the Father of our Lord Jesus Christ. In that day Israel will be included with Egypt and Assyria as a blessing in the midst of the earth, with the Lord of Hosts saying, *"Blessed be Egypt My people, Assyria My handiwork, and Israel My inheritance"* (Isa. 19:25b; see also verses 19-25a). The period of darkness that is coming over the whole world, including Israel and believers in Jesus Christ, will end in the glory of the Kingdom. The "until" stands as a guarantee of the new age for all, including Israel and Jerusalem.

Do we realize that we are on our way there? Perhaps our tent pegs would not be anchored so securely in this world were we to realize that as believers and the spiritual seed of Abraham we are on our way to that Promised Land, to His eternal Kingdom.

CHAPTER SEVEN

The Third "Until"—Until the Church Has Come In

I do not want you to be ignorant of this mystery, brothers, so that you may not be conceited: Israel has experienced a hardening in part until the full number of the Gentiles has come in. And so all Israel will be saved, as it is written: "The deliverer will come from Zion; He will turn godlessness away from Jacob. And this is My covenant with them when I take away their sins" (Romans 11:25-27).

Throughout the centuries, most Jews have not believed in Jesus as the Savior, although some might now consider Him to have been an important Jewish rabbi, though not the Son of God who died for the sins of the world, and thus also for the sins of Israel. Yet on the Day of Pentecost, some three thousand Jews believed and were baptized (see Acts 2:41). The birth of the Christian Church was exclusively a Jewish affair; those new believers in Christ were Jews and Gentiles who had converted to Judaism (see Acts 2:10-11). The disciples, the followers of Jesus, His friends who after the outpouring of the Holy Spirit become the sent ones (apostles), were all Jews. And it wasn't until Acts chapter 10 that we hear of the Holy Spirit being poured out upon non-Jews, Gentiles, when the Roman centurion, Cornelius, and all who heard Peter's proclamation of the Gospel, experienced the outpouring of the Holy Spirit in the same way as the Jews and proselytes (Gentiles who had converted to Judaism) did in Jerusalem during the feast of Pentecost. Peter and the believers from the circumcision (Jews who believed in Jesus) were astonished (see Acts 10:44-48)!

This unexpected conversion of the Gentiles sparked furious debate among Jewish Christians. Should the non-Jews, these Gentiles who now believed in Jesus, be required to keep the law of Moses and the 613 rabbinical commandments? Should they eat kosher? Had they in fact become Jews through their faith in Jesus? Must their men be circumcised? Should these converted Gentiles become observant Jews in every respect? Were they each a kind of proselyte? Because the Jewish Christians continued to observe the law of Moses, some demanded that the Gentile Christians do the same. What a shock it must have been to these new believers to be told that *"Unless you are circumcised...you cannot be saved!"* (Acts 15:1b). Your salvation is in jeopardy if you do not follow the Torah of Moses.

When those present with the apostles at the council in Jerusalem tried to come to terms with the problem of whether converted Gentiles, non-Jews who had come to faith in Jesus, should be expected to observe the law of Moses or not, the final conclusion was a resounding "No!" Peter said, *"Now then, why do you try to test God by putting on the necks of the* [Gentile] *disciples a yoke that neither we nor our fathers have been able to bear?"* (Acts 15:10). However, in order not to offend their Jewish Christian brothers and sisters, these Gentile Christians were asked to voluntarily, *"abstain from food polluted by idols, from sexual immorality, from the meat of strangled animals and from blood"* (Acts 15:20b; see also verses 19-20a). These were general rules that applied to strangers living in Israel (see Lev. 17:10-16), but the law of Moses was not imposed upon the Gentile Christians. It was sufficient that the law be upheld in the Jewish synagogue only.

There was thus an assumption that the synagogue would exist alongside the Christian Church. *"For Moses has been preached in every city from the earliest times and is read in the synagogues on every Sabbath,"* said James, the brother of Jesus (Acts 15:21). Both Church and synagogue have continued on through history, all over the world, but many times in a heartrending manner.

THE GOSPEL IS SPREAD FROM THE JEW TO THE GENTILE

The Lord had to do quite a lot of convincing before Peter, an observant Jew—and a Jewish Christian—was prepared to enter the house of Cornelius, the Roman Gentile. In fact, entering his house would have been regarded as defiling oneself. The Lord had to speak to Peter three times in a vision, telling him, *"Do not call anything impure that God has made clean"* (Acts 10:15b). In Peter's vision, he saw Heaven being opened and something like a great sheet being lowered by its corners. The sheet contained all kinds of animals, some clean and some unclean in terms of Jewish law. *"Then a voice told him, 'Get up, Peter. Kill and eat.' 'Surely not, Lord!' Peter replied."* (Acts 10:13b-14a). The vision was repeated three times before Peter understood that it was not about kosher food, but about kosher people (see Acts 10:9-23).

As he descended from the flat roof of the house where he had seen the vision, he met the messengers sent by Cornelius. They told him that an angel had instructed Cornelius to send for Peter and to hear a message from him, and they asked Peter to accompany them to Cornelius' house. Peter then understood that it was God's intention that he accompany them and thus, for the first time, the Gospel was proclaimed to the Gentiles—by a Jew.

This pattern of Jews preaching the Gospel to Gentiles was to continue. One might have expected that the Lord would haven chosen Cornelius to proclaim this message. After all, as a Roman, he was well acquainted with Greek and Roman thinking; he had become a believer in the Lord Jesus Christ, and was filled with the Holy Spirit, just like the Jewish believers in Jerusalem at Pentecost. Every director of a modern missionary society would undoubtedly have decided that such a man would be the most suitable person to appoint as the first apostle to the Gentiles. But instead, the Lord chose a Jewish rabbi, Saul of Tarsus, and revealed Himself to him in order to use him as the apostle to the Gentiles.

This is how God works. Salvation goes out to the whole world via Israel; salvation is from the Jews (see John 4:22). Saul became Paul, and the Lord Jesus appeared to him on many occasions. The first was at his conversion on the road to Damascus (see Acts 9:3-9; 22:3-16; 26:9-18) when he was still a confirmed Christ-hater, who pursued Christians, persecuted and imprisoned them (see Acts 9:1-2); was present when they were executed (see Acts 7:54–8:3); and thoroughly approved of it (see Acts 26:9-10). The Lord also appeared to him when he was alone in the desert, in preparation for his call to be an apostle. Later, he wrote about that time:

> But when God, who set me apart from birth and called me by His grace, was pleased to reveal His Son in me so that I might preach Him among the Gentiles [see Acts 9:15; 13:44-49; 22:21], I did not consult any man, nor did I go up to Jerusalem to see those who were apostles before I was [and thus I was not a student of Peter, or John, or James, so that my message came secondhand], but I went immediately into Arabia and later returned to Damascus (Galatians 1:15-17).

Later, Paul did visit Peter in Jerusalem for 15 days and also met James, the Lord's brother (see Gal. 1:18-19). But generally, Paul was unknown to the Christian community. They knew only that the one who had tried to destroy them was now preaching the Gospel! He had been changed from being a Christ-hater to one who proclaimed the Gospel.

EYE AND EAR WITNESSES

To qualify as a true apostle, one had to be an eye and ear witness of the Lord Jesus.

When the twelve disciples lost Judas through his betrayal of Jesus and his subsequent suicide, they chose a new twelfth apostle. The primary requirement for the position, which ultimately fell to Matthias, was to "have been with us the whole time the Lord Jesus went in and out among us, beginning from

John's baptism to the time when Jesus was taken up from us. For one of these must become a witness with us of His resurrection" (Acts 1:21b-22; see also verses 15-26). Similarly, the apostle John wrote: *"That which was from the beginning, which we have heard, which we have seen with our eyes, which we have looked at and our hands have touched—this we proclaim concerning the Word of Life…We proclaim to you what we have seen and heard…"* (1 John 1:1,3). He, too, was an eye and ear witness.

Paul, too, qualified as an apostle. Even though he did not accompany Christ during His lifetime in Israel, Christ did appear to him personally and instructed him, so that he did not learn his message from others but by revelation from God. He stated that his Gospel was not according to man, nor did he receive it from men, but through revelation of Jesus Christ Himself (see Gal. 1:11-12). The Lord went to great lengths with Paul to ensure the conversion of the Gentiles, the non-Jews, because He wanted it accomplished by a Jew.

The Great Commission of Jesus rings out: *"Go and make disciples of all nations* [the non-Jews, the heathens], *baptizing them in the name of the Father and of the Son and of the Holy Spirit, and teaching them to obey everything I have commanded you"* (Matt. 28:19-20a). He said this to His Jewish disciples, and as a result, the Gospel found its way into the whole world. At His ascension, He told His Jewish followers: *"You will be My witnesses in Jerusalem* [to Israel, the Jewish people], *and in all Judea and Samaria* [to the Samaritans, a mixed race, Jews who had mingled with other Gentile peoples during the deportation and exile of the ten tribes by the Assyrians—see 2 Kings 17:7-41; Ezra 4:19], *and to the ends of the earth"* (Acts 1:8b). The Gospel went from Jerusalem into the world in ever widening circles, and it was preached by Jews. They were the channels that God chose to use to bless the whole world.

LOVED BY GOD BUT REJECTING HIM NEVERTHELESS

Paul summarized the privileges of the Jews and stated, *"…Theirs is* [not: was] *the adoption as sons; theirs the divine glory, the covenants* [plural, for the old and the new covenant are sealed with Israel], *the receiving of the law, the temple worship and the promises. Theirs are the patriarchs, and from them is traced the human ancestry of Christ, who is God over all, forever praised! Amen*" (Rom. 9:4-5).

It is amazing how God works in the world through the Jewish people!

God did not choose Israel just for their own sake, or because they were greater, mightier, stronger, or more intelligent than other nations (although it is remarkable that such a small group has produced so many Nobel prize winners). On the contrary, Scripture states, "*The Lord did not set His affection on you and choose you because you were more numerous than other peoples, for you were the fewest of all peoples. But it was because the Lord loved you and kept the oath He swore to your forefathers...*" (Deut. 7:7-8). Even after Jesus was rejected by most of the Jewish people, Paul said of them that they were "*loved on account of the patriarchs, for God's gifts and His call are irrevocable*" (Rom. 11:28b-29).

Beloved of God. That is how God sees Israel, despite everything. So-called "unbelieving Israel" is loved by God.

And there's the rub. Paul knew that the Gospel is first for the Jew and also for the Greek (the Gentile, the non-Jew) (see Rom. 1:16; 2:9-10). And as an apostle, he consistently began his preaching and teaching in the synagogues, wherever his missionary journeys would take him. But he had to admit that for the most part, his "brothers after the flesh," his fellow Jews, refused to accept his message about Jesus. And he struggled with that. In fact, he wished himself "*cursed and cut off from Christ for the sake of my brothers, those of my own race*" (Rom. 9:3b). He strained himself to the uttermost "*in the hope that I may somehow arouse my own people to envy and save some of them*" (Rom. 11:14). It was an unceasing anguish in his heart (see Rom. 9:2). Why would they not believe? How could this be? What was the reason?

Then, gradually, or perhaps by a revelation from Christ, he began to see something. He discovered that God had a plan. By the end of the Book of Acts, he seemed to have stopped preaching to the Jews in hopes of their conversion and perceived the truth of God's statement in the Book of Isaiah:

"Go and tell this people: 'Be ever hearing, but never understanding; be ever seeing, but never perceiving.' Make the heart of this people calloused; make their ears dull and close their eyes. Otherwise they might see with their eyes, hear with their ears, understand with their hearts, and turn and be healed" (Isaiah 6:9-10).

"But that is not what I want," says the Lord to Isaiah in chapter 6. Paul adds, *"Therefore I want you to know that God's salvation has been sent to the Gentiles, and they will listen!"* (Acts 28:28).

Subsequently, Paul preached and taught openly and without hindrance about the Kingdom of God from his own rented house in Rome (see Acts 28:30-31). It seemed that communication with the Jews had ended. The schism between Church and synagogue was about to start. Salvation would now go directly to the Gentile world.

But there is something incomprehensible here. Even Isaiah felt it. Interestingly, Isaiah was commanded to prophesy and proclaim the message, lest they hear and understand and be converted—to preach in order that they would *not* hear, *nor* understand, *nor* believe, *nor* convert, *nor* come to faith!

*He said, "Go and tell this people: 'Be ever hearing, but never understanding; be ever seeing, but never perceiving.' **Make** the heart of this people calloused; **make** their ears dull and **close** their eyes. Otherwise they might see with their eyes* [but that is not what I want, says the Lord], *hear with their ears* [but that is not what I want, says the Lord], *understand with their hearts* [but that is not what I want says, the Lord], *and turn* [convert] *and be healed* [but that is not what I want, says the Lord]*"* (Isaiah 6:9-10).

Apparently, a partial hardening and rejection of Israel had to happen. It was to be so, for that was the will of God. A bewildered Isaiah then asked, *"For how long, O Lord?"* (Isa. 6:11a). And the Lord replied:

Until the cities lie ruined and without inhabitant, until the houses are left deserted and the fields ruined and ravaged, until the Lord has sent

everyone far away and the land is utterly forsaken. And though a
tenth remains in the land, it will again be laid waste. But as the tere-
binth and oak leave stumps when they are cut down, so the holy seed
will be the stump in the land (Isaiah 6:11b-13).

A portion would remain, which in the end (might) convert. This was
how the Lord was dealing with Israel.

Paul, quoting Moses (see Rom. 11:19) and Isaiah (see Rom. 11:20), says
in Romans 11:8, *"**God** gave them a spirit of stupor, eyes so that they **could not**
see and ears so that they **could not** hear, to this very day."* There was apparently
a plan of God behind all this, and ultimately, even Paul had to accept this
mysterious plan of God.

It is a two-sided puzzle. On the one hand, Israel (as a nation) rejected Jesus
as their Messiah and Lord, and therefore, God hardened the hearts of the majority of them. But on the other hand, Israel as a whole could not yet hear and
see, because God had other plans. Both guilt and fate are involved. A plan of
God is behind all of this. It is a mystery, Paul concludes (see Rom. 11:25), and
a mystery cannot be fully understood.

Jesus also knew that Isaiah's prophecy regarding the hardening of Israel
would be fulfilled. For that reason, He spoke to the Jews in parables; but to
His disciples, the chosen ones, He spoke clearly (see Matt. 13:10-17). Again
and again, there was a remnant in Israel who repented and did not bow their
knee to the Baals (see Rom. 11:4; 1 Kings 19:18). There has always been a
remnant according to the election of grace. But, finally, at the end of this period of world history, *all Israel*, having returned to their Promised Land, will
be saved (see Rom. 11:26)!

All Israel—the last generation before the Lord's return. And the rest of
Israel? Israel throughout the ages? Israel that was not without God but had a
blind spot for who Jesus is? If God has hardened and blinded them so that
they could not hear and could not see, did He by that act of His will con-
demn them also to everlasting and eternal rejection? We should that leave to
Him and not jump too quickly to "logical" conclusions of our own. He, the
God of Israel, is a God full of mercy.

The Third "Until"—Until the Church Has Come In

GOD'S INSTRUMENT OF SALVATION

Salvation comes in, by, and through Israel. First, the offer has been made to Israel, and a remnant responds; but many do not. *"Our forefathers were all under the cloud and that they all passed through the sea...They all ate the same spiritual food and drank the same spiritual drink...Nevertheless, God was not pleased with most of them; their bodies were scattered over the desert,"* says Paul about Israel (1 Cor. 10:1b,3-5).

Israel's experience is a warning to the Christian Church. Even if you were baptized as a child, attended a Christian school, experienced a Christian up-bringing, attended Sunday school and church, and studied catechism—all these are merely outward forms if your heart has not been given over to the faith. The circumcision of a Jewish male was meant to be more than a sign in the flesh; it was meant to represent "circumcision of the heart" (see Rom. 2:25-29). *"These people honor Me with their lips, but their hearts are far from Me* [sighed the Lord Jesus knowing God's heart and quoting the prophet Isaiah]. *They worship Me in vain; their teachings are but rules taught by men"* (Mark 7:6b-7; see also Isa. 29:13).

Superficially, one might say that it is Israel's own fault that God has punished and judged them, just as individuals today are personally responsible for rejecting the salvation that God offers to them. In other words, Israel is no different here than the rest of the world. But there is a deeper meaning in the hardening and rejection displayed by Israel. God is working through and by this hardening, to effect His salvation of the world, so that Israel has become a "negative instrument": *"Because of their transgression, salvation has come to the Gentiles...their transgression means riches for the world, and their loss means riches for the Gentiles"* (Rom. 11:11-12). Their rejection brings about the reconciliation of the world.

If so much good and salvation can stream into the world from their rejection, what will happen when Israel comes to fullness? *"How much greater riches will their fullness bring!"* (Rom. 11:12b; see also verses 11-15). Their hearts were hardened, made dull (see 2 Cor. 3:14a), so that we as Gentiles could come in. But when God gives the final revelation to Israel as well, how much more will the world be blessed by that!

DISPERSION OF THE JEWS—A BLESSING TO THE WORLD

The destruction of the city and the temple in A.D. 70 marked the starting point of the wandering of Israel all over the world. Moreover, this scattering of the Jews did much for the spreading of the Bible and the Gospel. In Jesus' days there were already many Jewish communities and synagogues scattered throughout the Roman Empire, from Babylon to Alexandria in Egypt and even in Rome. The apostles, and particularly Paul, always started their ministry in an area with an established synagogue, because they knew and could tell the Gentiles that in the synagogue was the Bible, and the knowledge of the one and only God, the Creator of Heaven and earth, YHWH, the covenant-keeping God of Israel, the God of Abraham, Isaac, and Jacob. And they could proclaim that this God is the Father of our Lord Jesus Christ, who died for the sins of the world and rose again, and is now sitting at the right hand of the Father, from where He will come again to establish His Kingdom as Messiah of Israel and King of the world.

All over the world synagogues sprang up as the Jews were scattered; and in the midst of all races, peoples, nations, and religions, the name and the Word of God, Moses, and the prophets were present in the synagogue. The representatives of the "root" in the form of the synagogue (Jewish congregations) apparently had to be physically present all over the world, in order that Gentiles might become engrafted, and join the covenant relationship of God with Abraham, by entering into the new covenant made by Jesus with the house of Israel and the house of Judah.

ENEMIES IN BOTH CAMPS FOR THE MESSIANIC JEW

Almost directly in their footsteps, Christian missionaries followed the scattered Jews and their synagogues, or sometimes vice versa, in a love-hate relationship, but standing together on the same root, the covenant with Abraham, extended into the new covenant, offered to Jew and Gentile. Yet the sufferings of the synagogue throughout the centuries as a result of Christian anti-Semitic theology and preaching have been indescribable. Persecution did not stop at words only—in Christian European countries the Jews were subjected to crusades, the Inquisition, pogroms, and the Holocaust.

A small group of converted Jews, Messianic Jews, Jewish Christians, baptized Jews, Christian Jews, or whatever we like to call them, have also long been part of the Church; but as Jews, they have often not felt at home in the Christian Church. Yet as "Christians," they have been shunned and considered traitors by their Jewish brothers and sisters. A Jew who converts to Jesus is no longer considered to be a Jew by his fellow Jews—in their opinion, this Jewish Christian has gone over to the enemy's camp, where the fate of the "unbelieving" Jew in the lands of Christendom has been quite horrible.

Indeed, missionary efforts among the Jews are looked upon by many rabbis as a form of genocide. They say that what Hitler was not able to accomplish with gas chambers, crematoria at Auschwitz, and the other concentration camps will be accomplished in a different way by missionaries. If they are successful, they will eradicate Judaism, they say. In the opinion of Orthodox Jews, Jews who become Christians stop being Jews, and hence, the Jewish people are diminished.

They are convinced that Jews becoming Christians (coming to Jesus and believing in Him as the Messiah of Israel and the Son of God, sacrificed as the Lamb of God for the sins of the world) are robbed of their Jewish souls. They consider Christianity as just another religion with more than one God, claiming, "You Christians believe that the Father is God and that the Son is God and that the Holy Spirit is God; and you even have a kind of goddess to whom you pray by the name of Mary."

Therefore Jews sometimes attempt to set up anti-missionary laws in Israel. But the Messianic Jews reply, "Not so, for it is through our faith in Jesus that we finally have become and feel like complete and fulfilled Jews!"

Of the 15 million Jews who are left in the world since the persecution and slaughters of the past centuries, five to six million live in Israel. Very serious reports tell us that about five to seven thousand of them are Messianic Jews, Jews who believe in Jesus, although not all of them are "full Jews." Some of them are married to non-Jewish husbands or wives. So, in Israel, only 0.1 percent believe in Jesus!

Another four to five million Jews live in the United States of America. Of those Jews some say that about 50,000 (or 1 percent) are Messianic Jews. Sometimes the percentage of "full Jews" who attend Messianic congregations is only 20 to 30 percent. The other 70 to 80 percent are Gentile Christians who love the Jewish style of the services. So today, about 99 percent of the Jews worldwide still don't believe in Jesus.

But there are those who do. And over the centuries, God has always given to some Jews the revelation about Jesus. These are the "firstfruits" as a guarantee of a great harvest that one day will come. This is the first reason why Paul speaks about "a hardening in part," in Romans 11:25. But there is a second reason as well—Jews are not without God, but they have a blind spot for who Jesus is. Again, compare Romans 9:4-5 with Ephesians 2:11-13 about what Gentiles have by birth and what Jews have by birth. Jews know God and God knows the Jews. I know that from personal experience.

A JEWISH MAN'S PRAYER

Many years ago, I suffered from a giant tumor of the brain. After the operation, the surgeon commented, "I have never seen a thing like that in my life! It was more or less the size of a grapefruit. I first had to cut bone from the base of your skull, where it had grown. Then I could see from upside down through your nostrils. My thought was, *There is really no use going on for this man, but I'll finish anyway.*"

Then he took bone from my hipbone and tissue from my thigh and placed them in the hole he had dug at the base of my skull. He also removed as much of the brain tumor that he and the team could find, cutting away some brain tissue; and then he shoved the brain back into position, closed the skull, and sewed me up. In addition, they put a drain in my spine to relieve pressure from the brain liquid in order to give the bone transplant a chance to settle; and after a week, they removed the drain. Subsequently, there was no leakage through the nose! I made a full recovery; praise the Lord!

At that time, I had already been involved for over 20 years in Christian radio and television production in the Netherlands. Many people in Holland knew me, because I had hosted many programs and shows. Consequently, half of Holland must have been praying for me. But what I did not know was what a Jewish man had done, whom I had met in Israel when working on a documentary about his impressive life story.

He had survived World War II, and was on the boat, the *Exodus*, that was turned away by the British from the shores of Israel. These Jews who had survived the concentration camps of Europe then ended up behind barbed wire at a concentration camp on Cyprus. Finally, he made it to Israel.

Although we had no further personal contact after the documentary, he apparently still had contacts in Holland. When he heard about my illness, he organized a "minyan," a group of ten Jewish men. (The existence of a Jewish congregation requires at least ten men who can pray. When there are no longer ten men, the congregation at the synagogue ceases to exist. Sorry, ladies, but this is how it is!) Then they travelled all the way from Tel Aviv to Jerusalem, to pray at the "Kotel," the Western Wall, that we sometimes call the Wailing Wall, where one can get as close as possible to the place where the holy temple once stood. When the temple was still there, the presence of God was in the holy of holiest of that temple. So, as closely as possible in the neighborhood of where God once dwelt, there they prayed for hours, until they had the inner conviction that this Christian man in Holland would live. Then they returned to Tel Aviv, and never even bothered to tell me about it!

Many years later someone asked me, "Do you know what Shlomo did when you had to go through your brain operation?" I said, "No…what?" Then he told me. Mind you, these were not Messianic Jews or Jewish Christians; these were devout, God-fearing, Orthodox Jewish men.

I fully recovered. Even the surgeon later wrote to me: "You are doing miraculously well, and I use that word on purpose, because I know what I did to your brain." This ended my career in radio and television. I then went back to the Universities of Groningen and Utrecht to complete my theological studies, and became an ordained minister in the Dutch Reformed Church, the national church of Holland. Then, years later, someone asked me to become the chairman of Christians for Israel.

So, after my life-threatening experience and a miraculous healing, the Lord led me to the Church on the one hand, and to Israel on the other hand, as if He wanted me to hold them both. Jews and Christians have been praying for my well-being, and God has answered them both. So I know from personal experience that Jews know God and God knows the Jews. He hears their prayers, listens carefully to them, and answers them. Although they have a blind spot for Jesus, Jews do know God.

"THE LORD OUR GOD, THE LORD IS ONE"

Despite the tension within the relationship of Church and synagogue, both share the same *root*, namely God's covenant relationship with Israel. More precisely, the Church stands on the root of God's relationship with Israel. Paul, speaking about an olive tree with a root and branches, had to remind the Roman Christians, *"You do not support the root, but the root supports you"* (Rom. 11:18b).

The root is the covenant of God with Abraham, with Israel, the revelation of His name YHWH, by which He connected with them, established His alliance with them (see Gen. 12:1-3; Exod. 4:13-15). YHWH represents the Lord in His covenant relationship, and is for that reason His greatest revelation to man. It is the eternal Torah, the eternally ever-present, creating Word, which was before creation, stemming from the Father—the Word that became flesh (see John 1:1-18). The root of Israel is the Word of God, the creating Word. That is YHWH in the old covenant; the Word made flesh, the Lamb of God in the new covenant. That is the Anointed One, the Messiah, and the King. *"I am the Root and the Offspring of David,"* He said (Rev. 22:16b; see also Rev. 5:5; Rom. 15:12). *"I am the way and the truth and the life. No one comes to the Father except through Me"* (John 14:6). *"Anyone who has seen Me has seen the Father"* (John 14:9b). *"I and the Father are one"* (John 10:30).

Again, the spiritual (and maybe even the physical) root of the Church is Israel, more specifically the new covenant made with the House of Israel and the House of Judah, part of the covenants God made with Israel. And this is still the case in spite of the early infiltration of the Church by elements of Greek philosophy and attempts to detach the Church from her Jewish root and to convert Israel to a non-Jewish theology. Despite her Gentile nature, the Church is grafted into the cultivated olive tree whose root is rich in sap (see Rom. 11:24). But the way we as Gentile Christians over the centuries have expressed our faith, cloaked in Greek philosophical terms that sometimes sounds like blasphemy to Jewish ears, has darkened the face of Jesus for them.

Let me give you just one example. Have you ever tried to explain the mystery of the Trinity to a Jewish person, using the words of the ancient Christian confessions of faith, which were deeply shaped by Greek philosophy? The eyes of your Jewish friend probably glazed over! Indeed, however hard you try to explain or grasp this mystery, it remains elusive. In the lands of Christendom over the centuries, Jews chose to die, burning at the stake, with the crucifix of Jesus right before their eyes, rather than accept this foreign Christian god and violate the basic confession of their Jewish, biblical faith: *"Hear, O Israel: The Lord our God, the Lord is One"* (Deut. 6:4). The concept of the Trinity is the basic stumbling block between Jews and Christians.

If asked about this matter by Jewish friends, I sometimes take the following approach: "You Jews believe that God is One, don't you?" "Oh yes, we do," they will probably reply. Then I say, "Did you know that Jesus, who was a pious Jew, also believed that? When He was asked what was the most important commandment of all (see Mark 12:28-34), He replied, *'Hear, O Israel; The Lord our God, the Lord is one,'* quoting the Shema (Deut. 6:4), known by every Jew and enclosed in the mezuzah on every Jewish doorpost. *'And love the Lord your God with all your heart, body, and soul'* (see Deut. 6:5-6; Mark 12:28-34; Lev. 19:18). The same answer that every observant Jew would give today."

The astounded response, "Did Jesus believe that?" reminds me how much we as a Church have clouded the face of Jesus for His own Jewish brothers and sisters. Then I say, "But you as Jewish people believe that the Torah is eternal and that God created everything through and by the Torah, don't you?" "Oh yes, we do!" "So He can do that, and still be one God, can't He?" "Of course, He can and He did," they would say.

"Now let us look at the things of creation," I say. "Let us look at the pillar of cloud and fire, and at the burning bush. These are all created things through which God could reveal Himself and still be one God, couldn't He?" "Oh sure," they will reply. "And what about the Angel of the Lord, who in Genesis 18:10 and 13 is called Lord, using the four unpronounceable letters of the name YHWH? Angels are created beings. So He can reveal Himself through the Angel of the Lord and still be one God, can't He?" "Oh sure," they will say. "Now then," I say, "if God wanted to reveal Himself in a perfect way to mankind, can He not, by the Torah through which He created everything, also create a human being in order to make God perfectly known to mankind, and still be one God? Cannot the Torah, in that sense as it were, become flesh, embodied in a human being, and God still be one God?" At this point, some will say, "Mmm, I never looked at it that way before. I have to think about that."

For a better understanding, in Judaism there are "hypostases" of God, five ways that God uses to reveal Himself in creation: "Metatron" ("Sar ha-Paniem, Sovereign Prince before the Face of God"); "Memra" ("Word" that comes forth from God); "Shekhinah" ("Divine Presence"); "Ruach ha-Kodesh" ("Holy Spirit") and "Bath-Kol" ("Voice from Heaven"). Whereas, Christians believe that the ultimate way God chooses to reveal Himself to this world is by incarnation in Jesus.

But no matter the differences in beliefs, one fact remains: The Church is grafted into that old root. The Church that reviled the synagogue and trampled Israel underfoot is merely an engrafted branch. Moreover, the Church has participated over the centuries in persecuting the true children of God even within her own ranks. The Church might, in the end, together with all other religions, even become part of an antichristian body as a new worldwide understanding of what religion is all about starts to arise: man being God, the religion of man. In the endtimes the apostate church herself will become part of a world-religious system that the apostle John calls the whore, drunk with the blood of the martyrs (see Rev. 17:6).

Drunk with the blood of Jew and Gentile.

ALL ISRAEL WILL BE SAVED

God will not ignore what has been done to His people. The period of grace for the Gentiles will someday end. However, in North and South America, Asia, and Africa, it seems that the period of God's grace is continuing, and many are coming to faith. Jesus promised that the Gospel would be preached to the ends of the earth before He returns (see Matt. 24:14). Through modern mass media, the Gospel is now going into the whole world, in all main languages, hundreds of hours per day, as never before in history.

At the same time, Israel is beginning to go home. Jesus predicted that as well. "*Now learn this lesson from the fig tree* [Israel]: *As soon as its twigs get tender and its leaves come out, you know that summer is near. Even so, when you see all these things* [happening], *you know that it* [the Kingdom of God] *is near*" (Matt. 24:32-33a; see also Luke 21:29-33). In addition, the signs of the times that He mentions in His end-time sermon (see Matt. 24; Mark 13; Luke 21) have been fulfilled over the last two thousand years, all except for two. And those two, the worldwide preaching of the Gospel and the return of the Jews to Israel, are being fulfilled in our day, before our very eyes. The return of Jesus is at the door! When God's work of grace among the Gentiles is completed, qualitatively and quantitatively, and the fullness of the Gentiles has come in, has been engrafted, then all Israel will be saved.

We are in the middle of a "cross-fade." The light over the heathen world is slowly fading, and the light over Israel is slowly coming on. All Israel shall be saved. What do we mean by "all Israel"? Do we mean that every Jew of the last generation living in Israel, before the coming of the Lord, will be saved?

Will all those people come to faith in Jesus? Every man, woman, and child? When this question was posed to Rebecca de Graaf van Gelder, a well-known Jewish believer in Holland, her response was, "What's the problem? Read Zechariah 12:10–14! Do you object to this? You should rejoice!" Paul says, *"And so all Israel will be saved, as it is written"* (Rom. 11:26a), and Zechariah says that all the generations, all the clans and their wives, yes, even the land, will mourn when they will look upon the One they (and we all) have pierced (see Zech. 12:10-14).

How is this going to happen? Keep on reading, for Paul refers to things happening *"as it is written"* (Rom. 11:26). How will it happen? he asks. *"As it is written."* The Greek phrase used here means "just as." Some people, however, stop reading after *"And so all Israel will be saved."* Then they explain that in this verse "all Israel" means the Church—all those Gentiles and Jews who believe in Christ—the "spiritual Israel." But this is a form of replacement theology, in which the Church is considered to be the "real" Israel, the newly chosen people of God, replacing the old unbelieving Israel. But there can be no doubt that in Romans chapters 9–11, Paul is speaking about physical Israel, not about the Church. *Israel* means Israel. He wrestles with the question of why most of the Jews cannot see who Jesus really is. And then he starts to see how one day they will, and he explains how finally all Israel shall be saved. So we have to read on.

This is how it will happen—as it is written! And what has been written? *"The deliverer will come from Zion; He will turn godlessness away from Jacob. And this is My covenant with them when I take away their sins"* (Rom. 11:26b-27) says God. He Himself will do that through the outpouring of the Holy Spirit and the return of Jesus.

There is in Scripture a clear line showing God working through Israel to reach the world, and not the other way around. Of course, in the future, in the Kingdom, the nations from all over the world will come to Israel and celebrate the Feast of Tabernacles in Jerusalem, bringing their gifts (see Zech. 14). Even today, people from all over the world help and support Israel, for instance, by upholding the Jews and helping them to return home. There is a practical line of assistance from the Gentile world to Israel; but is there a spiritual line as well? Yes, first and foremost, the Church in the nations has an obligation to pray for the Jews, for the nation of Israel, and for the peace of Jerusalem. And of course, we Gentile believers may receive the opportunity to present our Christian testimony to Jews as well. My Jewish friends sometime ask me about what I believe and why I do what I do, and are very interested as I share my personal testimony and explain my Christian faith the way I see it! Sometimes the Lord even blesses such testimonies worldwide by opening the eyes of Jewish persons to Jesus, so that he or she becomes a part of the "remnant according to the election of grace" (Rom. 11:5). But Scripture tells us that until Jesus comes, this will involve only a remnant, or the first fruits. Essentially, salvation of fallen mankind originates at the throne of God and goes via Israel into the world by the preaching of the Gospel. And my personal conviction based on the Scriptures is that one day it will come back to Israel again.

The mystery of Israel's unbelief is the mystery of the ingathering of the Gentile peoples. More accurately, it is the mystery of God's *"taking from the Gentiles a people for Himself"* (Acts 15:14b; see also verses 15-17), and then returning to *"rebuild David's fallen tent."* Then, through Jerusalem and Israel, salvation will go out from Jerusalem into a new earth. At first, there will be a Christian Church, a Bride for the Lamb, made up of Jews and Gentiles without any dividing wall (see Eph. 2:11-22), a Queen for the King. After that, all Israel will be saved and will be a blessing in the midst of the earth.

God will soon come to give Israel rest. Three times we have learned about a divine "until." Jerusalem is trodden underfoot by the Gentiles *until* the times of the Gentiles are fulfilled. Israel is temporarily and partially hardened *until* the fullness of the Gentiles, the fullness of the Christian Church (and only God knows when that point has been reached) has come in or has been engrafted into the root, into the new covenant made with Israel. And the Jewish people will not see Jesus *until* they will say, *"Blessed is He who comes in the name of the Lord."* And one day they will say just that.

Take note, as well, of the fig tree, which is even now beginning to sprout green leaves. The fulfillment of the divine "until's" is imminent. There is an urgency in our world. It is as if someone is speeding things up, compressing time. The Lord is making haste to fulfill His plan of salvation. It is a holy haste, for He knows that unless these days are shortened, no flesh will be saved (see Matt. 24:22; Mark 13:20). Make haste, therefore, to go to Him to be saved for time and eternity. Do it now while there is still time (grace)! Go down on your knees right now and give your life to Jesus.

CHAPTER EIGHT

The Root of Anti-Semitism

O God, do not keep silent;
be not quiet, O God, be not still.
See how Your enemies are astir,
how Your foes rear their heads.
With cunning they conspire against Your people;
they plot against those You cherish.
"Come," they say, "let us destroy them as a nation,
that the name of Israel be remembered no more."
With one mind they plot together;
they form an alliance against You
(Psalm 83:1-5).

To hate the Jews is to hate the God of the Jews. This emerges clearly from the psalmist's loud lament to Heaven, out of the depths of the misery of the Jewish people: "O God, do You not see it all? Of course, You do; but Oh God, do not remain silent. Rouse Yourself, and do not remain idle. This is not just about our enemies, God; they are Your enemies as well. They hate You. They devise an attack against Your people, because that is who we are—Israel, Your people. They want to strike Your protégés, and so it involves You. They want to pierce Your heart. How do they intend to do that? By destroying Your Jewish people, so that the name of Israel will be forgotten."

The greatest enemies suddenly become friends when they unite against Israel, just as Herod and Pilate became friends on the day they condemned Jesus. Prior to that day, they had been enemies (see Luke 23:12). The psalmist lists the enemies of Israel as *"Edom and the Ishmaelites, of Moab and the Hagrites* [descendants of Hagar], *Gebal, Ammon and Amalek, Philistia, with the people of Tyre. Even Assyria has joined them..."* (Ps. 83:6b-9). There is nothing new under the sun. As soon as Israel reappears on the world stage in the Middle East, her enemies unite against her. Large enemies like Syria, Iraq, and Iran (part of the former Assyrian Empire), smaller enemies like the Palestinians (who view themselves as the descendants of the Philistines, and pronounce the name "Palestine" as "Philistia"), those living in Jordan (Edom, Moab, and Ammon), and in the kingdoms of the Arabian Peninsula (the Ishmaelites) join together despite other dissensions, united in their hatred of Israel. Suddenly, the Arab League agrees on unanimous verdicts and measures. "For they have conspired together with one mind," says the psalmist; but he clearly sees beyond the immediate when he continues, *"They form an alliance against You."* The battle is between the God of Israel and other gods of this world. That is what the hatred for Israel is ultimately all about.

For Israel is a designated sign of God in the world. When one of the German Kaisers once asked a famous theologian for proof of the existence of God, he thought for a moment and then said, "The Jews, Sire!" No other people on earth has been so persecuted and destroyed, and nearly annihilated, and still remains a recognizable people. No matter how often Israel has tried to assimilate and join the surrounding nations in the world, it has never succeeded. If Israel herself did not always want to be distinct, her enemies made sure that she was. For centuries when they lived in strange surroundings, often barely aware of their own Jewishness, those around them knew exactly who was a Jew and who was not. Hitler's henchmen knew exactly how to trace them. In Russia and in its satellite countries, people filled with a fiery hate for the Jews knew where to find them.

Demonic powers fuel the hatred for the Jews, using people for their own ends (yet even though those who persecute the Jews still remain responsible for their deeds). It is the great enemy of God and humanity—the devil—who in the Bible is called a *"murderer from the beginning,"* the *"father of all lies"* (see John 8:44), who directs his hatred of God onto the people of God. And when hate "rains" on the Jewish people, "raindrops" also fall on the Christians…at least on those who remain true to the Bible. It was so under Hitler and under Stalin and Russian communism. Right-wing fascists, national-socialist dictators, and left-wing communists might be fierce opponents ideologically, but they are united in their hatred of everything to do with God and the Bible. *"They form an alliance against You,"* the psalmist says. Hatred of Israel is hatred of the God of Israel.

THE GODS OF EGYPT

Hatred of Israel has been a reality since the beginning. It was there when Israel originated as a people, when famine forced Jacob's sons to migrate to Egypt, where they grew into a strong nation. Joseph's contribution was forgotten and the Egyptian pharaohs enslaved them. The Pharaoh said to the Egyptians, *"Come, we must deal shrewdly with them…So they put slave masters over them to oppress them with forced labor, and they built* [the cities of] *Pithom and Rameses…"* (Exod. 1:10-11). The Egyptians *"worked them ruthlessly. They made their lives bitter with hard labor in brick and mortar and with all kinds of work in the fields; in all their hard labor the Egyptians used them ruthlessly"* (Exod. 1:13-14).

Their slave labor was hard, and the pressure on them was systematically increased, motivated in part by the economy and in part by hatred. Then the murders began. All baby boys were to be killed at birth by the midwives. When that order was ignored, instructions were issued that every boy born was to be thrown into the Nile, but every daughter to be kept alive (see

Exod. 1:15-22). Later, the slave labor became even more arduous; they were no longer given straw to be mixed with clay to make bricks, but would have to gather the straw themselves, while still producing the same quota of bricks (see Exod. 5:1-21).

The sufferings became nearly intolerable, and then God stepped in. Moses was rescued from the waters of the deadly Nile by an Egyptian princess (see Exod. 2:1-10) and raised at the court of the Pharaoh—a divine irony—where he was instructed in all the wisdom of the Egyptians (see Acts 7:22). Later, he was spiritually molded during his 40 years in the wilderness, before being called to lead the people of Israel in the great Exodus from Egypt. But first, he had to do battle with the gods of Egypt in ten plagues, when Israel also needed to learn who the Lord was.

Many years later, Ezekiel, speaking in the name of the Lord, said,

This is what the Sovereign Lord says: On the day I chose Israel, I swore with uplifted hand to the descendants of the house of Jacob and revealed Myself to them in Egypt. With uplifted hand I said to them, "I am the Lord your God." On that day I swore to them that I would bring them out from the land of Egypt into a land I had searched out for them, a land flowing with milk and honey, the most beautiful of all lands [see Exod. 6:1-8] *And I said to them, "Each of you, get rid of the vile images you have set your eyes on, and do not defile yourselves with the idols of Egypt. I am the Lord your God"* (Ezekiel 20:5-7).

While in Egypt, Israel served the gods of Egypt. Joshua, Moses' successor, later challenged the people of Israel with his stirring call:

Now fear the Lord and serve Him with all faithfulness. Throw away the gods your forefathers worshiped beyond the River [the Euphrates river, on the far side of which Abraham, the father of Israel, had served the local gods before God called him] *and in Egypt, and serve the Lord. But if serving the Lord seems undesirable to you, then choose for yourselves this day whom you will serve, whether the gods your forefathers served beyond the River, or the gods of the Amorites, in whose land you are living. But as for me and my household, we will serve the Lord* (Joshua 24:14-15).

But the people did not respond, for as God tells Ezekiel:

But they rebelled against Me and would not listen to Me; they did not get rid of the vile images they had set their eyes on, nor did they forsake the idols of Egypt. So I said I would pour out My wrath on them and spend My anger against them in Egypt. But for the sake of My name, I did what would keep it from being profaned in the eyes of the nations they lived among and in whose sight I had revealed Myself to the Israelites by bringing them out of Egypt. Therefore I led them out of Egypt and brought them into the desert. I gave them My decrees and made known to them My laws, for the man who obeys them will live by them (Ezekiel 20:8-11).

All around Israel, and often with Israel at stake, the battle played out between God, YHWH the Lord, and the false gods. Which specific false gods did God battle in Egypt? We can tell the answer from the plagues. The first of the ten plagues was directed at the Nile, which was worshipped as Hapi, the giver of life. The waters of the Nile turned to blood. The Nile had been the grave of many Jewish baby boys; now it ceased to be a source of life for the Egyptians. Its waters turned poisonous and became undrinkable; the fish died and everything stank. What a humiliation!

The plague of frogs humiliated the god Hektor, a representation of the god Hathor.

The plague of mosquitoes and gnats was directed against Isis, the wife of Osiris, and the revived Hathor, one of the most important Egyptian goddesses, who was worshipped in the form of an ox. Both people and cattle suffered. The pestilence on the livestock and the plague of boils were aimed at Ptah (or Apis), the bull god of Memphis, as well as at other gods who took the form of cattle, goats, or sheep.

Serapis was the god of protection against locusts, but was helpless when the plague of locusts attacked Egypt.

And then came the thick darkness.

The supreme god of the Egyptians was the sun god, Ra. But Ra was unable to drive back the dark. Pharaoh himself was regarded as the son of Ra; however, when the tenth plague took his firstborn son (and all the firstborn sons in Egypt), the divine Pharaoh was revealed to be powerless (see Exod. 7:14–11:10).

All these plagues made it quite clear that Egypt's man-made gods could not save. Egypt's religion, which imparted divine properties to nature, could protect neither man nor beast, nor the firstborn sons of the Egyptians.

But the Jewish boys in the land of Goshen remained alive. Israel's children had been murdered, but now it was evident who was Lord. The blood of the slaughtered lamb applied to the doorposts and the lintel protected the people of Israel in the land of Goshen in Egypt (see Exod. 12:1-30). (The use of the blood of a lamb points to Christ, the Lamb to be sacrificed for the sins of the world, to avert God's anger from sinful lost people who have placed their hope on Jesus.) When the people fled from Egypt, the waters of the Red Sea were divided by a strong east wind, and Israel traveled safely across; but the Pharaoh and his horsemen perished (see Exod. 13:17–14:31).

OTHER FALSE GODS

Thereafter, when dealing with His people Israel, the Lord revealed Himself to the peoples of the world and to Israel itself. Repeatedly, He demonstrated who the true God really is. When the Israelites reached Moab, Balaam, who saw the children of Israel drawing closer and had heard about their great exploits and victories over enemies, was invited to come and curse Israel. Even though he would have liked to use his demonic and occult powers to do so, he was powerless against the God of Israel. In spite of himself, he had to bless them, rather than curse them (see Num. 22:2–24:25). *"How can I curse those whom God has not cursed? How can I denounce those whom the Lord has not denounced?…I see a people who live apart and do not consider themselves one of the nations*" ["*…and shall not be reckoned among the nations*"—KJV] (Num. 23:8-9).

Yet Israel fell into idolatry again and again. When Moses stayed away too long, the golden calf was erected and worshipped as the goddess Hathor, one of the Egyptian gods. Even in the Promised Land, after the Lord had given victory over the Canaanites, with their horrible idols requiring child sacrifice and temple prostitution, Israel fell into idolatry and worshipped those same gods—Moloch, the Baals, and Astarte. They worshipped creation rather then the Creator, and that is idolatry. To worship nature and to seek out the world of the demonic is idolatry. The person who serves and exalts himself instead of his Maker practices idolatry. And idolatry draws God's irrevocable wrath (see Rom. 1:18-32).

And time and again the Lord showed who He really is.

When Israel was in exile in Babylon, Nebuchadnezzar, the destroyer of the temple in Jerusalem, had to bow down to the God of Israel (see Dan. 4). The idol had to make way for the worship of the God of the Jews (see Dan. 3).

The Persians, such as Haman, also had to learn what happens to haters of Jews, and to all who want to destroy the Jewish people. Israel continues to annually celebrate the feast of Purim and reads the Book of Esther to recall that the great destruction that Haman had planned was foiled. At the feast, the Jewish children eat special cookies—Haman's ears!

It is interesting to note that the great anti-Semite, Haman, was a descendant of Amalek, who had opposed Israel in the desert (see Esther 3:1,10). He was in the direct line of Agag, the king whose life was spared by Saul, against the express order of the Lord, until Samuel himself stepped in (see 1 Sam. 15). Balaam also mentions Agag (see Num. 24:7); and the Septuagint, which is the Greek translation of the Old Testament, translates his name as Gog. Ezekiel says that Gog will again be an important figure in the endtimes, as an enemy of Israel (see Ezek. 38–39; Rev. 20:8). Then he, too, will be destroyed. Haman/Gog are types of anti-Semites and antichrists.

PHASES OF DESTRUCTION

Pharaoh, Agag, Haman, Gog...the line of anti-Semites is long and enduring. The greatest so far has been Hitler, who systematically increased the pressure and, like Pharaoh, adopted "policies."

- Phase 1 (1933): Nazis administered and plundered Jewish stores, boycotted Jewish businesses, and regularly maltreated Jews.

- Phase 2 (1935): The Nuremberg laws against the Jews were passed.

- Phase 3 (1939): There were mass arrests of twenty thousand Jews, with the first use of systematic physical violence and the first mass deportations to the concentration camps. Before 1939, a Jew could still buy his way out of Germany with loose change; after 1939, it cost him all his wealth, and even then, he could barely escape.

- Phase 4 (1940): All German and Austrian Jews were deported to the ghettos in Poland.

- Phase 5: The *Endlosung* (Final Solution). First came the murderous units, the *Einsatzgruppen* (special units following the *Wehrmacht*, carrying out mass executions). After 1941 (coinciding with the invasion of Russia), the concentration camps and work camps became slaughterhouses, abattoirs. Millions of Jews were murdered. Technical advances (such as the Zyklon-B gas) increased the tempo of destruction to its maximum.

The end result was at least six million Jews (the exact number can never be determined) were murdered, including one and a half million children. A person was murdered...six million times, frequently in a most inhumane and cruel way. Words fail us.

The Aryan super race rose up against the people of God, whom the Nazis considered "Untermenschen" (people at the lowest level of human evolution, less than rats). They were used as rats, or guinea pigs, in atrocious human medical experiments. They were considered evolutionary misfits who should be destroyed in the interests of human progress toward becoming *Übermensch* (superman). Darwin had introduced the concept of the survival of the fittest, meaning the survival of the strongest. Hitler (like Karl Marx, the founder of communism) was a great admirer of Darwin. Hitler was not the source of the idea of a superior race; that idea had already existed for decades and had been developed at the German universities. It was argued that evolutionary progress came about through combat, in which stronger animals destroyed weaker, less well-adapted species. This model justified the destruction of any *Untermensch*, who were obstacles to the development of a superhuman race. Besides the Jews, the mentally deficient, the disabled, homosexuals, gypsies, and other groups of "Untermensch" were also destroyed.

In whatever way hatred is ideologically clothed, it is ultimately hatred of God. It is hatred of the Creator of Heaven and earth. It is hatred of the people He has chosen in order to reveal His will in the world through them. It is hatred of the great Son of the Jewish people, Jesus Christ.

Unlike the Calvinists, who see man as by nature hostile to God and his neighbor, Jews generally have an optimistic view of human nature, regarding people as a mixture of good and evil. Humanism, too, teaches that man is essentially good and any evil elements can be overcome by providing better living conditions and more education. Faced with the rise of Nazism, the Jews repeatedly believed that things would eventually improve, that the good in people would eventually regain the upper hand. Hitler had laid out his views on the Jews and their ultimate fate in his book, *Mein Kampf*, but most Jews never dreamed it could become a reality, and with such speed. And so they remained in Germany until it was too late and they could no longer leave.

CHRISTIAN HATRED

Hatred of the Jewish people has also been preached by a false form of Christianity as a legitimate hatred of the "God-murderers," the "God-killers." But Jesus Christ, the Lamb of God who takes away the sins of the world, laid down His life of His own free will (see John 10:18), and on the cross He had prayed, *"Father, forgive them, for they do not know what they are doing"* (Luke 23:34a).

A form of Christian theology, or perhaps one should rather say anti-Christian theology, has for centuries held the Jewish people collectively responsible for the death of Jesus. The Church has been less merciful than God. It cannot be repeated often enough that the crusades, inquisitions, pogroms, and Holocaust took place in the Christian world and represent Christian anti-Semitism. Even today, the World Council of Churches issues one pro-Palestinian pronouncement after another and one pro-Palestinian declaration after another.

Whereas, the Roman Catholic Church today issues all kinds of good and positive statements about the Jewish people and makes careful speeches about Christian anti-Semitism in the past. They sometimes have a better attitude towards the Jewish people and Israel today than many Protestant churches and the World Council of Churches do. But yet, they did not totally acknowledge the State of Israel for many years. The visit of Pope John Paul II to Israel in 2000 and the words of repentance he spoke there were a good starting point for a better relationship. But words have to be followed by deeds.

Joseph Cardinal Ratzinger, at age 78, was chosen on April 19, 2005, by the cardinals of the Roman Catholic Church to be the next Pope, the 265th successor of the apostle Peter, bishop of Rome and head of the universal Church, as they see it. Pope Benedict XVI made a promising start when he immediately connected with the Chief Rabbi of Rome, and with every visit he continues to openly declare the special role and position that the Jewish people have in the eyes of God.

However, replacement theology, the teaching that the Church has replaced Israel as God's chosen people, has been preached for centuries and has seeped deep into the veins of Roman Catholic, Protestant, and Eastern Orthodox theology, as we have realized in previous chapters. According to this theology, when the majority of the Jews did not accept Jesus, the Church came to be seen as the new people of God. In this view, the Church receives the promises of Scripture, while curses and judgments are set upon the Jewish people and Israel. This teaching is alive and well, and very popular among Arab and Palestinian Christians, who thus have little difficulty in sharing the hatred and condemnation directed at Israel by their Islamic Arab brothers.

But hatred of Israel is hatred of the God of Israel. Christian hatred of Israel, though robed in theological terms, is still hatred of God. Nowadays, many point to the seeming change in the thought climate in the Christian world toward Israel. But just how far that change will go remains to be seen. It is possible that the best years of theological new thinking are already behind us.

After the Second World War, there was a readiness in Europe to adopt a changed attitude, including a changed theology, toward the Jewish people and Israel. The Dutch Reformed Church in the Netherlands (de Nederlandse Hervormde Kerk, today the Protestant Church of the Netherlands, PKN) played a prominent role in this, but over the past few years there has been a change in this church too. On the international level and as a member of the World Council of Churches, the Dutch Church often stood alone in her support of Israel, asking for special attention for Israel and her unique place among the nations in God's eternal plan of salvation, like a voice crying in the wilderness.

But then other forms of theology emerged. Higher Bible criticism, eroding the reliability of the Scriptures, had paved the way for that. Theology of the revolution. Theology of the poor. Theology of the emancipation and liberation of women. God is with the underdogs, these theologies claimed. Despite some good social and humane aspects of these horizontal and social types of theologies, some basic things were often overlooked. The Bible as the ultimate authority itself suffered from it. The preaching of the Gospel suffered from it. The unique position of Christ and the expectancy of His coming in glory suffered from it. And today, the Palestinians are being portrayed as the underdogs, and theological thinking has turned to a Palestinian "liberation theology." There is no special place for Israel in this kind of Christian theology, and no place to consider the developments in the Middle East in biblical prophetic perspective! No special place for Israel!

God sees it otherwise. He is faithful to His covenants with Israel. And now, Israel is on the way to rest for her body, soul, and spirit. The reborn Jewish State is an undeniable fact. In Israel, Jews can be themselves. Spiritually, many of them are rediscovering their Jewish roots. The number of synagogues in Israel is growing, as is the degree of Jewish awareness. There, in the Promised Land, God's Spirit will be poured out on them, as foretold by the prophets Joel, Jeremiah, Ezekiel, and Zechariah. Then Jewish souls will be totally at rest and rejoice in the salvation that the God of Abraham, Isaac, and Jacob, the Father of our Lord Jesus Christ, will pour out upon them and in them, by His grace. Then Israel will live safely in the midst of the earth and will be a blessing to the nations.

For God did not choose Israel solely for Israel's own sake, but because He wanted, through Israel, to bless the whole world. And He will not forsake what His hand has begun. He will come to give Israel rest.

CHAPTER NINE

The Land of Israel

He is the Lord our God;
His judgments are in all the earth.
He remembers His covenant forever,
the word He commanded, for a thousand generations,
the covenant He made with Abraham,
the oath He swore to Isaac.
He confirmed it to Jacob as a decree,
to Israel as an everlasting covenant:
"To you I will give the land of Canaan
as the portion you will inherit"
(Psalm 105:7-11).

AN ETERNAL COVENANT

These are impressive words. The eternal God made an eternal covenant with Abraham, Isaac, and Jacob, and with Israel, their descendants. The Lord has made a solemn oath.

When we take an oath, we use the words, "So help me God," sometimes with one hand on the Bible and the other raised toward Heaven. A more serious declaration cannot be made, and perjury is severely punished. The Lord cannot swear by anyone higher than Himself, for no such person exists, so He swears by Himself: *"By Myself I have sworn, My mouth has uttered in all integrity a word that will not be revoked"* the Lord says to Isaiah (Isa. 45:23). And to Jeremiah He says, *"But if you do not obey these commands, declares the Lord, I swear by Myself that this palace will become a ruin"* (Jer. 22:5). In a psalm the Lord says, *"Once for all, I have sworn by My holiness—and I will not lie to David"* (Ps. 89:35).

When God makes an oath, it is absolutely trustworthy. He made a solemn oath to Abraham (see Gen. 12:1-3; 17:4-8), and Isaac (see Gen. 26:2-5), and Jacob (see Gen. 28:13-15; 35:9-12), and an eternal covenant with Israel when He said, *"To you I will give the land of Canaan as the portion you will inherit"* (Ps. 105:11).

What does the word *eternal* mean? Only until Jesus Christ came and the Jews rejected Him? When a portion of the Jewish people rejected Jesus, declaring, *"We don't want this man to be our king"* (Luke 19:14b) did the eternal covenant suddenly dissolve? No, of course not. Eternal means eternal, everlasting, forever. That covenant is still valid today.

What was the content of this everlasting covenant, based on a solemn oath that God had sworn by Himself? *"To you I will give the land of Canaan."* That was what God said to Abraham in Genesis 12:1–3, and repeated to Isaac and Jacob, and on numerous other occasions. "It is My land," said God (see Lev. 25:23), "and I give it to you, to Israel."

Was the land uninhabited when the Lord promised it to Abraham? No. It was inhabited by the Kenites, the Kenizzites, the Kadmonites, the Hittites, the Perizzites, the Rephaites, the Amorites, the Canaanites, the Girgashites, and the Jebusites (see Gen. 15:13-21; Deut. 7). Yet God still gave the land to Israel.

Did He Himself see to it that before Israel took possession, those peoples had willingly moved on? Did Israel enter an empty land? No. Israel had to conquer the Promised Land. In order to achieve that objective, Moses' successor, Joshua, under whose leadership the people of Israel would enter the land after wandering in the desert for 40 years, had to be strong and very courageous. Many times he and the people of Israel were told, *"I will give you every place where you set your foot, as I promised Moses"* (Josh. 1:3; see also Deut. 31:1-8,23; Josh. 1:1-9). This promise meant that Joshua had to be courageous himself, to go in faith and put down the soles of his own feet. Faith is like that. If you go out in faith and obedience, you will find that you will possess the land. But you have to do it yourself. It will not just be tossed into your lap.

JUDGMENT IN SPITE OF COVENANT

Why was the land of Canaan taken away from the heathen peoples who lived there? It was because the measure of their wickedness was full (see Gen. 15:16; Deut. 9:3-6). God's judgment was passed on those peoples. At times, Israel was not even allowed to leave anyone alive; at other times, not even material possessions could be taken as booty, as was the case at Jericho, where the gold, silver, and articles of bronze and iron were declared to be holy (separated unto the Lord) (see Josh. 6:17-19). When Achan took some for himself, he became the reason for Israel's first humiliating defeat at Ai (see Josh. 7:1-5). It was only after Achan's family (who apparently agreed with the theft) was killed (see Josh. 7:6-26) that Israel could conquer Ai (see Josh. 8:1-29).

But just as God punished the wickedness of the nations in Canaan, so He punished the wickedness of Israel. Moses warned them:

If you do not carefully follow all the words of this law, which are written in this book, and do not revere this glorious and awesome name—the Lord your God—the Lord will send fearful plagues on you and your descendants…Just as it pleased the Lord to make you prosper and increase in number, so it will please Him to ruin and destroy you. You will be uprooted from the land you are entering to possess. Then the Lord will scatter you among all nations, from one end of the earth to the other (Deuteronomy 28:58-59;63-64a; see also 28:60-68; 11:22-32; 12:29-32; 8:19-20).

Israel's history demonstrates that punishment was enforced several times. The ten tribes of Israel were taken into Assyrian exile (see 2 Kings 17:20-23) and the two tribes of Judah into Babylonian captivity (see 2 Kings 25:8-12). A remnant remained in Judah (see 2 Kings 25:22), and after 70 years, some of the Jews who had been taken to Babylon (42,360 to be exact—see Ezra 2:64) returned to Israel (see Ezra 1–2). But large Jewish communities remained in the Diaspora (the scattering). Jerusalem and the temple were rebuilt after the Babylonian exile, and for several centuries existed in relative independence. But when the Romans finally took over and destroyed the temple and the city, Israel once again went into exile—this time worldwide, as Moses had foreseen (see Deut. 28:64).

But does that invalidate the eternal oath and the everlasting covenant that God had sworn to Abraham, Isaac, and Jacob? No! Yet the Church for centuries has claimed that it does! When God makes an eternal covenant, it is an eternal covenant. He does not go back on His word. He is absolutely trustworthy. The Old Testament contains numerous references to the eternal oath that He has sworn and the pledges He Himself has made to Israel and His promise to give them the land of Canaan (see Exod. 6:7-8; 13:5,11; 32:13; 33:1; Num. 14:30; Deut. 1:8;34-35; 6:10,13; 7:8,13; 8:18; 9:5; 10:11; 11:9,21; 19:8; 26:3; 28:11; 30:20; 31:7; Josh. 1:6; 21:43-45). Israel may plead for that.

THE MIRACLE

God made a promise to Israel, and Isaiah called on Israel to hold God to His promise:

And give Him no rest till He establishes Jerusalem and makes her the praise of the earth. The Lord has sworn by His right hand and by His mighty arm: "Never again will I give your grain as food for your enemies, and never again will foreigners drink the new wine for which you have toiled; but those who harvest it will eat it and praise the Lord, and those who gather the grapes will drink it in the courts of My sanctuary" (Isaiah 62:7-9).

This has been the prayer of Jewish people over the ages at Pesach, the Jewish Passover, when they pray, "Next year in Jerusalem!"

That prayer remained unfulfilled until 1948, when the miracle happened. On May 14, 1948, David Ben-Gurion called the independent State of Israel into being. Prior to that date, on November 29, 1947, the United Nations had adopted a plan for the partition of Palestine. As soon as that plan was announced, the powerful Arabs embarked on a ferocious battle to drive the Jews into the sea and nip the new Jewish State in the bud. Despite heavy losses, the Jews prevailed. This bloody conflict and British opposition to the plan (aided and abetted by the Arabs) led the United Nations to propose the dissolution of the partition plan. But within six months, before the plan was revoked, David Ben-Gurion proclaimed an independent Jewish State. The last British troops left the country the next day, the same day on which seven Arab nations attacked Israel. By a divine miracle, the unequal battle went in Israel's favor, and thus early in 1949 an armistice was declared. However, Egypt had conquered the Gaza strip, and Jordan had occupied the West Bank and East Jerusalem; and they refused to turn the armistice into a peace.

British Opposition

Britain's role in all this was dubious, and often downright anti-Semitic. To Britain's credit, it must be said that it had adopted the Balfour Declaration in 1917, in which the right of the Jewish people to a "national home" in Palestine was acknowledged. But when Britain was assigned a mandate over Palestine after the First World War, ending four hundred years of Turkish occupation, the British increasingly supported the Arabs. The British military in Palestine pitted Arab and Jew against each other. As early as 1923, London had secretly decided to use political and economic means to crush Zionism. The first British High Commissioner to Palestine, Herbert Samuel, in 1922 approved the establishment of Trans-Jordan as a region which would not form part of the future national Jewish home. In 1923, the British declared that Trans-Jordan would be autonomous, and the land division was actually carried out in 1928. A major part of the biblical Promised Land was simply cut off and given to the Arabs.

Early in 1919, the Arab National Congress in Damascus had made Syria and Iraq into two separate states, so that the map of the Middle East gradually assumed its modern shape. In 1945 the Arab League was founded, and Jordan became a member. On March 22, 1946, the British recognized the Arab League and granted Jordan total independence. And then in 1948, Jordan, along with troops from Egypt, Syria, and Iraq, attacked the new State of Israel.

Israel was back on the world stage, but so too were Israel's enemies. Britain's role just prior to the Second World War is painful to recount. Even before the war, Jewish synagogues were burning in cities all over Germany, torched by the Nazis and the inflamed German people. Initial reports of the existence of concentration camps were also beginning to filter through. Anyone who had read Hitler's book, *Mein Kampf*, could discern what was going to happen to the Jews. And yet on May 17, 1939, London decided to limit Jewish immigration to Palestine to 75,000 persons. The High Commissioner was instructed to block all Jewish land acquisition, and a plan was drawn up for an independent administration within ten years. This plan would have ensured that the Jewish people would always remain a permanent minority in Palestine, their future Jewish national home.

While under the satanic regime of Goebbels, a half million Jews were mistreated, starved, left without home, work, or hope, and hence, were trying to escape to Palestine; yet the British government simply treated them as "illegal immigrants." Britain maintained this policy throughout the war, despite what was happening to the Jews under the Nazi regime. Even after the fall of Hitler, British soldiers were instructed to shoot those human wrecks, almost skeletons, who having barely escaped the concentration camps were trying to enter Palestine. The Arabs in Palestine rejoiced over the destruction of the Jews by Hitler. The Grand Mufti of Jerusalem (the leader of the Muslims there), Husseini, was a personal friend of Hitler; and Britain chose to back the Mufti and his men (who regularly murdered Jews in pogroms in Jerusalem and in the rest of the Arab world) and to go against Jewish interests. In spite of the horrors of the Second World War, the British forced the surviving Jews to remain in the concentration camps and sank boats that tried to reach the coast of Palestine illegally. Those Jews who did not drown but managed to swim ashore were picked up by the British and placed in new concentration camps on Cyprus. Patriotic Jews in Palestine were hung.

Between 1947 and May 1948, hundreds of Jews were murdered on the roads and in the fields of Palestine each month, while the British turned a blind eye to the Arab murderers and would not permit the Jews to be placed in convoys for safety.

NOT WIPED OFF THE MAP

In 1948, the newly born State of Israel was immediately attacked by the surrounding Arab nations. Their armies, which enjoyed the help of the British High Command, included:

- ❖ Four thousand men in the armies of North Palestine, Syria, and Iraq.
- ❖ Four thousand mercenaries and Bedouin in an army from East Palestine, recruited in Trans-Jordan under the eye of the British army.
- ❖ Three thousand men in an army from West Palestine which occupied Tel Aviv and the road to Jerusalem.
- ❖ Ten thousand men in the extremely strong and well-equipped Egyptian army in the south.

As Israel was being born, under the eyes of British soldiers, these armies took control of the vital Haifa-Tel Aviv road, isolating the kibbutzim in the Negev. They totally isolated the Jewish people in Jerusalem and the kibbutzim in the south near Bethlehem. They were in a position to attack Tel Aviv and cut off the roads to Jerusalem and to the kibbutzim in the south. When the British handed over the mandate in Palestine, they left their military posts, handing them over, often with all their weaponry, to the Arabs. The situation of the Jews appeared hopeless.

The Arab League ordered the local Arabs to leave Israel while they were quickly finishing off the Jews. "In two weeks you will be able to return, for then all the Jews will be dead and everything will belong to you." They were warned, "If you remain there as an Arab, you might be killed."

This order was the start of the Palestinian refugee crisis. The Jews did not create it; the Arabs themselves did. For the Jewish State did not get wiped off the map in two weeks.

It seemed unbelievable, that a nation of 600,000 Jews could survive an attack orchestrated by leaders of the 45 million enemies who surrounded them. The word "miracle" was on everyone's lips. The Lord fought on the side of His people, as in the days of the Old Testament.

We will not go into detail about the events of 1956 when shortly after nationalizing the Suez Canal, President Nasser of Egypt declared that he was ready to deal with the "Jewish problem" once and for all. Israel retaliated, crossed the Sinai desert, and soon stood at the edge of the Suez Canal. In the baggage of the Arab soldiers who had been taken prisoners, they found dozens of copies of *Mein Kampf*, translated into Arabic.

In 1967, exactly on the 19th anniversary of Israel's independence, Nasser again brought his tanks into the Sinai, closed the Gulf of Aqaba and threatened to use his air force to bomb Jewish cities. The Israeli air force launched a daring surprise attack that destroyed the entire Egyptian air force on the ground. Jordan was defeated; the West Bank of the River Jordan (which Jordan had occupied since 1948) and East Jerusalem were returned to Israeli possession. For the first time in nearly two thousand years, Jerusalem was again the undivided capital of Israel, a Jewish State.

THE START OF REDEMPTION

In 1973, on the Day of Atonement, the most holy day of the Jewish calendar, Syria and Egypt attacked. Israel sustained great losses, but did gain the victory. Yet the nation was deeply shocked. How much more Jewish blood would have to flow before there would be real peace? The answer can only be given when the Messiah has come. Even since the peace process in the Middle East has begun, hundreds of Jews have been murdered by Arab Islamic fundamentalists. And the end is nowhere in sight.

What about Jerusalem?

The pressure to divide the city in some way in order to give the Palestinians their own "capital" continues to mount, while the Christian world pushes for the internationalization of Jerusalem. How do you think the Italian government would respond if this were to be proposed for the city of Rome?

This is not meant to be a book on politics or history, but when you look at the situation of the Jewish State of Israel—now in existence for more than 50 years—from a biblical perspective, you cannot overlook the historical and political situation. One thing is certain—the miracle of the mere existence of Israel continues even in its recent history. It should be impossible, and yet Israel continues to exist. Because the Lord said, *"To you I will give the land of Canaan, as the portion you will inherit"* (Ps. 105:11), Israel is on the way to her rest. But before that rest can become a reality, many things will happen, and most of them unpleasant.

But the "beginning of the deliverance" as the rabbis call it, the forming of a Jewish State and the return of the Jewish people to Israel, has begun; and it is an irreversible process. The prophet Amos says, *"'I will plant Israel in their own land, never again to be uprooted from the land I have given them,' says the Lord your God"* (Amos 9:15). Ezekiel promises in God's name: *"Then they* [Israel] *will know that I am the Lord their God, for though I sent them into exile among the nations* [already fulfilled], *I will gather them to their own land, not leaving any behind"* (Ezek. 39:28).

Israel is here to stay. They will not be uprooted again.

DIMENSIONS OF THE HOMELAND

What, according to the Bible, are the borders of the Promised Land? The answer is more global than specific. From the river of Egypt (Wadi el

Arish, the eastern branch of the Nile) to the Great River, the Euphrates (see Gen. 15:18). The area from the Red Sea to the Sea of the Philistines (the Mediterranean Sea) and from the wilderness to the Euphrates (see Exod. 23:31). From the wilderness of Zin as far as Rehob, where the road to Hamath starts (see Num. 13:21). *"...the hill country of the Amorites...all the neighboring peoples in the Arabah, in the mountains, in the western foothills, in the Negev and along the coast, to the land of the Canaanites and to Lebanon, as far as the great river, the Euphrates"* (Deut. 1:7). From the wilderness to Lebanon and from the river Euphrates as far as the western sea (see Deut. 11:24). From the entrance of Hamath to the brook (wadi) of Egypt (see 1 Kings 8:65; 2 Chron. 7:8). From the entrance of Hamath as far as the Sea of the Arabah (see 2 Kings 14:25). From the river Euphrates to the brook (wadi) of Egypt (see Isa. 27:12).

What is striking here are the recurring references to the Euphrates. Is this river to be the northern or eastern boundary, or both? If the Euphrates is to be the eastern border, then the Lord has promised a large area east of the Jordan! If the Euphrates is to be the northern border, then Syria (Aram) also belongs to Israel, but the area to the east might be limited. Although it is reported that during the entry into the Promised Land, the tribes of Reuben, Gad, and the half-tribe of Manasseh settled beyond the Jordan, this has not always been accepted without discussion (see Num. 32; Josh. 13:8-33; 18:7; 22:1-4;9;25; Deut. 3:16-18). Various descriptions in the Bible seem to assume that the Jordan is the eastern border of the Promised Land of Canaan (see Num. 32:29-42; 34:2-12; 35:10; Deut. 32:47; Josh. 22:9-11), meaning that the Euphrates is viewed as the northern border (thus including Syria and the Golan Heights). Mention is also made of Gilead, the northern portion of the land beyond the Jordan, which is also promised to Israel: *"I will bring them to Gilead and Lebanon, and there will not be room enough for them"* (Zech. 10:10b; see also Jer. 50:19). *"Benjamin will possess Gilead"* (Obad. 1:19-20).

The division of the land described by the prophet Ezekiel is yet another story. In chapters 40 to 48 he speaks of the temple, and describes it in great detail. According to some, this temple seems to be situated not in Jerusalem, but in the area where Shiloh was once located, that is, the place where the tabernacle first came to rest after the trek through the wilderness. The area of the Promised Land is also defined (see Ezek. 47:15-20; 48:1,28). A survey of the data leads some to conclude that the heart of the Promised Land and the temple will be to the west of the Jordan; and that once the final temple has been built and is in place, the Euphrates will indeed be the northern and eastern border.

WHAT ABOUT GAZA?

Sometimes people ask, "Gaza, does it really belong to the Promised Land?" The answer is, "Yes!" The Bible clearly says so. Just like the Golan. Sometimes people say, "But I cannot find the Golan in the Bible, besides it being the name of a city." The reason for that is the Romans named this part of their occupied province *Gaulanitis*, or Golan. The Bible calls it *Bashan*, and it was undoubtedly part of the Promised Land (see Deut. 3:12-20; Josh. 13:8-13; and other Scriptures).

"Ekron, with its surrounding settlements and villages; west of Ekron, all that were in the vicinity of Ashdod, together with their villages; Ashdod, its surrounding settlements and villages; and **Gaza**, *its settlements and villages, as far as the Wadi of Egypt and the coastline of the Great Sea* [the Mediterranean]*"* (Josh. 15:45-47). So the Jews who voluntarily left Gaza for the time being, will be back. Read Zephaniah 2:4-7.

Likewise, Judea and Samaria are part of the Promised Land, although today people refer to them as the "occupied territories," or the "West Bank." They are even the heartland of Israel. After King Solomon, the ten tribes named "Israel" lived in the area of Samaria, with their capital the city of Samaria; and the two tribes named "Judah" lived in the area of Judea, with Jerusalem in between.

The Lord God made an everlasting covenant when He promised all the land of Canaan to Israel. We have already mentioned Psalm 105:7-11, but let's look at it again:

*He is the Lord our God; His judgments are in all the earth. He re-
members His covenant forever, the word He commanded, for a **thousand generations**, the covenant He made with Abraham, the oath
He swore to Isaac. He confirmed it to Jacob as a decree, to Israel as an
everlasting covenant: "To you I will give the land of Canaan as the
portion you will inherit."*

Sometimes a *generation* means 40 years, sometimes 70, or even 100
years. So, for 40,000 years or even 70,000 or 100,000 years, the Lord means
this covenant to last. Indeed, it lasts "forever": it is an everlasting covenant.
What does *everlasting* mean? Until Jesus Christ and then no more? That is
what the Church has sometimes said and even today still says, considering
herself to be the "new Israel," the "spiritual Israel"—although one cannot
find these expressions in the Bible. But in any case, *everlasting* means forever!

The prophet Jeremiah even says in chapter 31:35-36: *"This is what the
Lord says, He who appoints the sun to shine by day, who decrees the moon and
stars to shine by night, who stirs up the sea so that its waves roar—the Lord
Almighty is His name: 'Only if these decrees vanish from My sight,' declares the
Lord, 'will the descendants of Israel ever cease to be a nation before Me.'"* So as
long as Heaven and earth, the universe and the laws of nature exist, Israel
will not cease to exist. Never. And Israel's "sins" do not change that. Read the
next verse, Jeremiah 31:37, as well.

Let us next look at some of the important places in this part of the land of
Israel. Although today, parts of the land are called the "occupied territories," or
the "West Bank," these areas are part of the Promised Land. They are the biblical lands of Judah and Samaria. Let us consider the rich history of some of
the cities in order to realize what an importance they are for Israel today. One
might even number some of these cities among the "holiest" cities of Israel.

HEBRON

A very important city for Israel is Hebron. Its location is 35 kilometers
south of Jerusalem, with vineyards and orchards. The city was given to Caleb

(see Josh. 14:6-15), who together with Joshua gave a positive report about the Promised Land (see Num. 13). Hebron, also named Kiriath Arba, is the city where Sarah died and is buried (see Gen. 23:2,19). Here also Isaac died (see Gen. 35:27-29); and here Abraham, Isaac, and Jacob are buried (see Gen. 49:29-33), as well as Rebecca and Leah—in the cave in the field of Machpelah, near Mamre, which Abraham bought as a burial place from Ephron the Hittite, along with the field (see Gen. 50:12-14). This is the city where all the patriarchs of Israel and their wives are buried.

In the 19th century, a large Jewish population lived in Hebron. Then in 1929, a massacre by the Arabs took place, and in 1936 the Jews left. But today, there is again a Jewish settlement—or rather village—at Hebron, Kiriath Arba, often ferociously attacked by the Arabs.

The city of Hebron was founded seven years before the city of Zoan in Egypt (see Num. 13:22), probably around 1700 B.C.. The descendants of Anak (see Deut. 2:10; 9:2; Josh. 11:22) lived here: Ahiman, Sheshai and Talmai, giants in the eyes of the Israelis (see Num. 13:22). Then Caleb drove them out (see Josh. 15:13-14).

Here Abraham pitched his tents and lived (see Gen. 13:18). Then the Lord appeared to him and promised him the birth of a son of his own, and Sarah laughed (see Gen. 18:1-15). It was called the city of a king (see Josh. 12:10). And when Joshua conquered the city, he killed the king (see Josh. 10:22-28;36-39). Afterwards, Hebron became one of the cities of refuge (see Josh. 20:7). It was a city assigned to the descendants of Aaron (see Josh. 21:9-13).

David was king here for seven years and six months (see 2 Sam. 2:1-4;11). Abner was killed here (see 2 Sam. 3:22-27). The head of Ish-Bosheth was buried here (see 2 Sam. 4:12); and David had Ish-Bosheth's murderers killed here. In Hebron, the tribes of Israel anointed David to be king (see 2 Sam. 5:1-5). His son Absalom was born here (and five other sons) (see 1 Chron. 3:1-4), and here Absalom rebelled against his father (see 2 Sam. 15:10). Later Rehoboam fortified the city (see 2 Chron. 11:5-12).

After the return from the Babylonian captivity, the city was inhabited again (see Neh. 11:25). Later, Edomites were driven away by the Judas Maccabeus (see 1 Maccabees 5:26). The Romans destroyed the city during the Jewish wars, around A.D. 70, Flavius Josephus tells us.

During the times of the Byzantines, a Christian church, a basilica, was built over the cave of Machpelah, and during the Arab occupation, Machpelah became an Islamic shrine as well. Today, it is a unique place, serving as a shrine for Muslims and Jews alike—both a mosque and a synagogue…until the bloodbath in recent years by a man named Goldstein.

SAMARIA

Samaria is the name for a whole area, with cities, high places, and temples (see 1 Kings 13:32, 2 Kings 17:26). It was a place of much crime and apostasy (see Hos. 7:1). It is also the name of a city—Samaria (see 1 Kings 16:23-24), the capital of the kingdom of the ten tribes of Israel. It is a beautiful area, Isaiah 28:1-6 says. But there are several "woe's" against Samaria, as there are against Jerusalem (see Mic. 1:5-6).

Excavations have found the remnants of palaces of Omri, Ahab (a palace inlaid with ivory), Jeroboam, and Ahazia. Ahab was buried here, and there was a water reservoir (see 1 Kings 22:37-39). In addition, Amos prophesied its judgment (see Amos 3:9-15).

In 722 B.C., Shalmaneser of Assyria captured and ransacked the city and deported the Israelites to Assyria (see 2 Kings 17:5-6; Hos. 10:14), because of Israel's sins (see 2 Kings 17:7-23). He transported other people to other parts of Samaria (see 2 Kings 17:24-40). So the Samaritans became a mixed population. Elijah and Elisha (see 1 Kings 17–19, 2 Kings 1–13) had warned the Israelites and their kings against their serving the idols, the Baals. Jehu listened (see 2 Kings 10) and destroyed Baal worship in Israel. The reformation under King Josiah was also in this area (see 2 Kings 23:19).

Alexander the Great established a colony here with Macedonians, and the city became hellenized. Johannes Hyrcanus conquered it for the Jews.

The Romans then took it back and gave it to the Samaritans. Augustus gave the city to Herod. And being who he was, Herod built great buildings at Samaria. Its Greek name was Sebastos, and Herod called it Sebaste. The Arabs later called it Sabastiya.

To this very day, there are about 500 real Samaritans living with their own version of the five Books of Moses and their own sacrifice at Pesach. They are descendants of the mixed population that was formed after the transportation of the ten tribes of Israel into Assyrian captivity.

Here is Mount Ebal, 941 meters high, north of Shechem, where Joshua built an altar. Here also is Mount Gerizim, and here Joshua copied the law of Moses (see Josh. 8:30-34).

And one day (today), Israel will live on the mountains and hills of Samaria, plant their vineyards there, and enjoy the fruit of them (see Jer. 31:1-6), as well as in the land of Judah (see Jer. 31:23-30).

Shechem

The town of Shechem is located between Mount Ebal and Mount Gerizim. Abraham built an altar here (see Gen. 12:6-7). Jacob pitched his tent here, bought the place and built an altar for the Lord (see Gen. 33:18-20). Here Jacob's sons Simeon and Levi took revenge on behalf of their sister Dinah (see Gen. 34). Joseph was sent by this father to Shechem and sold by his brothers to the Midianites, who in turn sold him in Egypt to Potiphar (see Gen. 37:12-36). Later, Joseph was buried here (see Josh. 24:32). In recent years, we have witnessed the total desecration of this place by Islamic Arab nationalists. At first, they set fire to the place—Joseph's grave, a Jewish shrine; then they changed it into a mosque.

Under Joshua, here the covenant with the Lord, the God of Israel, was renewed (see Josh. 24:1-27). Here the history of Abimelech took place (see Judg. 9). Jeroboam lived here (see 1 Kings 12:25). Today the old city itself is a tell in the neighborhood of Nablus.

SHILOH

In Shiloh, Joshua set up the tabernacle and cast lots for the tribes to distribute the land to the Israelites in the presence of the Lord (see Josh. 18:1-10; 19:51). During the time of the judges, the house of God was in Bethel (see Judg. 20:26-27), and later again in Shiloh (see 1 Sam. 1:3; 4:3-4)—the first place that He made a dwelling for His Name (see Jer. 7:12).

From here the Israelites took the ark and brought it to the battle with the Philistines (see 1 Sam. 4). Then the ark went from Ebenezer to Ashdod—*"the glory has departed from Israel, for the ark of God has been captured"* (1 Sam. 4:22). Then the ark went to Ekron, then to Beth Shemesh, then to Kiriath Jearim. Then it was moved by David to Mount Zion (see 2 Sam. 6)—the city of David; and from there, Solomon brought up the ark and placed it in the temple (see 1 Kings 8:1). Here in Shiloh, Hannah received the promise that she would have a son named Samuel (see 1 Sam. 1), and dedicated him to the house of the Lord.

I have always wondered why in Jacob's blessing for Judah (see Gen. 49:10 KJV), it is stated, *"...until Shiloh come..."*—although the NIV translates, *"...until He comes to whom it belongs..."*—referring to the ruler's staff. The NIV refers to Ezekiel 27:21 and Numbers 24:17. But could it also mean that the temple of Ezekiel chapters 40–48 will be located in Shiloh, after the whole landscape of the Jerusalem area has been changed by the earthquakes? (See Zechariah 14:3-4 and Revelation 11:13.) The Mount of Olives will split, and undoubtedly the rest of the mountains around Jerusalem will change as well! So there might still be an important role for Shiloh in the future!

We could go on and on to speak about other places in Samaria and Judah, such as Bethel, Bethlehem, and Gibeon—all cities in these areas that today are called the "occupied territories." But nevertheless, this land of Samaria and of Judah is the heartland of Israel, with Jerusalem in the middle. It is here that almost all the history of the Old Testament took place. This is the land of the Bible. This is the land of the histories of the kings of Israel and Judah, the land of all the prophets of Israel. This is the land from "Dan to Beersheba" (see Judg. 20:1; 1 Sam. 3:20; 2 Sam. 3:10; 17:11; 24:2,15; 1 Kings 4:25; 1 Chron. 21:2; 2 Chron. 30:5); the land that Abraham had to walk, from north to south, from east to west (see Gen. 13:14-17); and that was promised to him and to Israel with an everlasting promise, an everlasting covenant made by the eternal God.

LEARNING TO TRUST

What is all this leading up to?

In the first place, we realize that Israel does not exist by the grace of the United Nations, or by the grace of the United States of America, or of Russia, or Europe, or by the grace of Christianity or Islam; but Israel exists by the grace of God on the basis of an everlasting covenant. Furthermore, the Lord is true to His everlasting covenant with Israel. Even though the borders of the land are not totally clear, the problem as seen from a biblical perspective is not the West Bank (the West Bank has always belonged to the Promised Land) but the East Bank, and thus Jordan and Syria. These could also become part of Israel. And after the coming of the Messiah who will usher in true world peace—perhaps as a pre-fulfillment of the promises of the Kingdom of God that in the end will consist of a new Heaven and a new earth—there might yet be even more territory, reaching as far as the Euphrates on the northern and eastern borders.

What political "rights" can Israel derive from these biblical promises right now?

The answer is for Israel to decide. For far too long, the Jews have lived in circumstances and countries where they have been told precisely what they as Jews are allowed to do or not do. Israel is a free country, which has politically chosen a Western democratic model of government, in contrast to the Arab dictatorships around them. Thus, in the first place, the decision belongs to the Jewish people. If one looks at the debates continuing in the Knesset—Israel's democratic Parliament in Jerusalem—one sees all the political positions from the (ultra) left to the (ultra) right being hotly debated. They really don't need outsiders like us to tell them what to do. They are able to make their own decisions in a very democratic way.

Furthermore, it is remarkable that Israel ever accepted the United Nations plan of division in 1947, when the Arab nations rejected it! Especially in light of the fact that all the aggressive wars that neighboring nations have launched to annihilate the Jewish State and drive the Jewish people into the sea have actually led to expansion of Israeli territory. It is interesting to note that throughout history, European countries fought colonial wars that enlarged their territories. Yet Israel, by contrast, has carried out defensive wars rather than colonial ones. And then to call Jewish pioneers in underdeveloped areas "settlers" certainly gives a negative flavor (intentional?), which is encouraged by the Western media, who often provide a one-sided, pro-Palestinian and pro-Arab picture of developments in the Middle East.

In truth, Israel wants peace and is prepared to take great risks, even to the extent of exchanging land for peace.

But do the other parties really want peace? Or is this "peace process" of today just another form of waging war by the Palestinians and the Arabs? Are they practicing "salami tactics," trying to gradually take over the whole land of Israel, slice by slice? Time will tell. One thing is certain—Israel must learn to trust the God of Abraham, Isaac, and Jacob. That has become plain to the world, after considering the conflicts in the Middle East over the past 60 years. The world saw the God of Israel fighting at the side of His people, so that the modern-day small David was victorious over overpowering, surrounding Goliath-nations. The Lord is with His people. Israel can and should trust Him for that, and not boast about their own mighty military strength.

But at the same time, the Jewish people themselves need to be strong and courageous, and continue to develop a well-trained army—as in the days of Joshua, when they were told by the Lord to place the soles of their feet on the Promised Land and thereby experience the blessing of the Lord. He will give it to them, and His giving will be experienced by them as they proceed in faith. If Israel chooses to rely solely on its weapons or on clever international politics, the words of the Old Testament prophets will apply, as they repeatedly warned against trusting in alliances with Egypt, or Assyria, or Babylon. Their warnings were well founded, for the great powers surrounding Israel eventually turned against her. But when Israel trusts in the Lord, there will be blessing, prosperity, peace, and victory over the threatening enemies.

Israel is on the way to her rest. The Lord will come to give Israel rest, even though the way might yet be long. It will end only with the coming of the Messiah, the return of the Lord Jesus Christ, and the coming of His Kingdom. *"There will be great distress, unequaled from the beginning of the world,"* Scripture declares (Matt. 24:21a); but after that there will never again be such a time of tribulation. The Lord will again rescue them out of *"a time of trouble for Jacob"* (see Jer. 30:7-9). He will not abandon what His hand has begun. With all our unfaithfulness, He remains faithful. That is our, and Israel's, only hope. And then, finally, there will be blessing also for the surrounding nations and a highway from Egypt to Assyria. All these nations will serve the Lord, and Israel will rank third among them, says the Scripture (see Isa. 19:23-25).

What about the Palestinians today? Do they have biblical rights as well?

Listen to the words of the prophet Ezekiel:

> *"You are to distribute this land among yourselves according to the tribes of Israel. You are to allot it as an inheritance for yourselves and for the aliens who have settled among you and who have children. You are to consider them as native-born Israelites; along with you they are to be allotted an inheritance among the tribes of Israel. In whatever tribe the alien settles, there you are to give him his inheritance,"* *declares the Sovereign Lord* (Ezekiel 47:21-23).

So the land remains Israel's, and there should not be an independent Palestinian state on Israel's Promised Land with its own army and all that that entails.

Although some rabbinical expositors argue that this text applies to non-Jews who have become proselytes (that is, Gentiles who by conversion have become Jewish), the text does not specifically say so. It could very well include genuine strangers, such as the Palestinians, who could personally possess some part of the land, like a house or an orchard.

But the land itself is Israel's, and has been promised by the Lord to the Jewish people with an everlasting covenant. And the strangers who live in it must abide by Israeli law.

Israel has full biblical rights to possess the whole of the Promised Land, including some of the East Bank, even without reference to the borders during David and Solomon's reigns, sometimes called Greater Israel by certain political commentators. Were we simply to stick to the boundaries of the Promised Land under Joshua, after the Exodus from Egypt, Israel should include the Golan (the biblical Bashan), Judea and Samaria, the West Bank, and possibly even a small part of the East Bank. And Jerusalem should be the undivided capital of the State of Israel. The only place for an independent Palestinian state would be in Jordan, or somewhere else in the Arab world.

CHAPTER TEN

Jerusalem and the Temple

But you will cross the Jordan and settle in the land the Lord your God is giving you as an inheritance, and He will give you rest from all your enemies around you so that you will live in safety. Then to the place the Lord your God will choose as a dwelling for His Name—there you are to bring everything I command you: your burnt offerings and sacrifices, your tithes and special gifts, and all the choice possessions you have vowed to the Lord. And there rejoice before the Lord your God, you, your sons and daughters, your menservants and maidservants... (Deuteronomy 12:10-12).

When Israel recaptured Jerusalem in 1967, the hearts of devout Jews began to beat faster. Would this be the moment when the temple could be rebuilt, and if so, where?

But what is it, that is so special about Jerusalem?

The Lord has decided to make it a dwelling for His name. The eternal God, Creator of Heaven and earth, has chosen to live there. There is His holy mountain (see Isa. 11:9; 56:7; 65:11,25; Zeph. 3:11), Mount Zion (see Joel 2:1; 3:17), where God has fixed His dwelling place (see Ps. 74:2). There is the house of the God of Jacob (see Isa. 2:3), the house of the Lord (see Ezek. 8:14,16; Joel 1:13-14; Mic. 4:1-2; Hag. 1:14).

The song that Moses sang after the miraculous crossing of the Red Sea during the exodus from Egypt, also established the place of His dwelling: *"You will bring them in and plant them on the mountain of Your inheritance— the place, O Lord, You made for Your dwelling, the sanctuary, O Lord, Your hands established"* (Exod. 15:17). Later, he told the Israelites to *"rejoice before the Lord your God at the place He will choose as a dwelling for His Name—you, your sons and daughters, your menservants and maidservants, the Levites in your towns, and the aliens, the fatherless and the widows living among you"* (Deut. 16:11). Yes, there is room in the temple even for the stranger, as is clear from King Solomon's dedicatory prayer:

> *As for the foreigner who does not belong to Your people Israel but has come from a distant land because of Your name—for men will hear of Your great name and Your mighty hand and Your outstretched arm—when he comes and prays toward this temple, then hear from heaven, Your dwelling place, and do whatever the foreigner asks of You, so that all the peoples of the earth may know Your name and fear You, as do Your own people Israel, and may know that this house I have built bears Your Name* (1 Kings 8:41-43).

THE SYMBOL OF GOD'S PRESENCE

Initially, the presence of God was strongly associated with the ark of the covenant (see Exod. 25:10-22)—the chest that contained the two stone tablets with the Ten Commandments written on them by the Lord Himself (see Exod. 31:18; 34:1,27-28; 1 Kings 8:9), a jar of manna (see Heb. 9:4; Exod. 16:33-34), and Aaron's rod that budded (see Num. 17:8-10). On top of the ark was a mercy seat of pure gold with two cherubim, figures of angels, also of pure gold. The faces of the cherubim were turned toward the mercy seat where the high priest sprinkled the blood of sacrifices. The ark of the covenant represented the Lord enthroned among the cherubim in Heaven (see Isa. 6:1-4; Ezek. 1; Rev. 4), just as the entire tabernacle was a representation of the heavenly model (see Exod. 25:8-9).

The ark, which contained God's holy law, and thus symbolized God's holy law on earth, causing people to fear His judgment, was also the throne of grace for sinful people when the blood of innocent sacrifices was sprinkled on the mercy seat. The holy law was covered with sacrificial blood. In a sense, all those animal sacrifices under the old law received retroactive validity through the completed work of Christ, the perfect sacrificial Lamb. The blood of sacrificial animals could only temporarily cover the sins of Israel (see Heb. 10:4-10); whereas, the blood of Christ obtained eternal redemption (see Heb. 9:11-15). The law, the ark, and the sacrifices were at the heart of Israel's religion; and the Lord was enthroned upon the cherubim on the ark, His footstool (see 2 Sam. 6:2).

The ark travelled with the Israelites in the wilderness; and once they reached the Promised Land, it was kept first at Shiloh (see Josh. 18:1), then in Beth Shemesh (see 1 Sam. 6:1-21), then in Kiriath Jearim (see 1 Sam. 7:1), then for three months in the house of Obed-Edom (see 2 Sam. 6:10-12), and then finally was brought to Jerusalem. The ark is also mentioned as having been carried into battle during the reign of David (see 2 Sam. 11:11; 1 Chron. 28:2; Ps. 99:5; 132:7; Lam. 2:1), but King Josiah decreed that it was to remain in the temple (see 2 Chron. 35:3).

After the destruction of Jerusalem and the temple by Nebuchadnezzar of Babylon, the ark is never heard of again; and prophesying the return of Israel, the recovery of Jerusalem, and the rebuilding of the temple, Jeremiah says that it will never be made again: *"In those days, when your numbers have increased greatly in the land, declares the Lord, men will no longer say, 'The ark of the covenant of the Lord.' It will never enter their minds or be remembered; it will not be missed, nor will another one be made"* (Jer. 3:16). But with or without the ark, the temple on Mount Zion, in Jerusalem, which is also named the Holy City, is the dwelling place of the Lord (see Isa. 48:2; 27:13; Neh. 11:1,18; Ps. 24:3).

THE POSSESSION OF JERUSALEM

It took some time before the people of Israel actually understood what Jerusalem was all about and possessed the city as their own.

> *On that day the Lord made a covenant with Abram and said, "To your descendants I give this land, from the river of Egypt to the great river, the Euphrates—the land of the Kenites, Kenizzites, Kadmonites, Hittites, Perizzites, Rephaites, Amorites, Canaanites, Girgashites and Jebusites..."* (Genesis 15:18-21).

This land was not an empty land, but inhabited by various peoples. One of those groups, the Jebusites, lived in Jerusalem.

According to the Lord, Joshua had to be strong and courageous and place the sole of his foot upon the Promised Land, and then the Lord would give the land to Israel (see Josh. 1:1-9). Israel had to walk in faith, and in the process of going, they would experience the truthfulness of the promises of God. But there were times when Joshua and the Israelites did not do what God had instructed, and instead, they allowed some people who already lived in Canaan to remain alive and stay there (see Josh. 3:10-11; compare 11:22; 16:10; 17:12-13; 19:47).

For example, Israel had planned to eventually conquer Jerusalem, but Adoni-Zedek, king of Jerusalem, thought he had a better plan. After hearing about the successful conquests of the Israelite army, He joined forces with the other four kings of the Amorites to fight the Gibeonites at Gibeon. Through deception, the Gibeonites had made a peace treaty with Joshua and the Israelites (see Josh. 9), and they were now calling upon Joshua to help them face the forces of the Amorite kings. Joshua and the Israelites marched from Gilgal to Gibeon, and won the battle (see Josh. 10). After the battle, he killed and hung the five Amorite kings, including the king of Jerusalem (see Josh 10:22-25); yet apparently, he did not conquer Jerusalem. For later, in Joshua chapter 15, we read, "...*Judah could not dislodge the Jebusites, who were living in Jerusalem; to this day* [the writer of the Book of Joshua says] *the Jebusites live there with the people of Judah*" (Josh 15:63). And that, apparently, remained the case for the next couple hundred years. Even after the conquest by the men of Judah (see Judg. 1:8), the Israelites left the city, so the Jebusites returned (see Judg. 1:21). The city was even named after them—Jebus (see Judg. 19:11-12; 1 Chron. 11:4).

This is remarkable. Although Israel conquered the Promised Land and divided it among the 12 tribes, they still didn't acquire Jerusalem—not until David became king over Israel, after Saul. In Second Samuel 5:6-10 and First Chronicles 11:4-9, we read how the Jebusites were finally overcome. *"David was thirty years old when he became king, and he reigned forty years. In Hebron he reigned over Judah seven years and six months, and in Jerusalem he reigned over all Israel and Judah thirty-three years"* (2 Sam. 5:4-5).

This is a striking parallel to Israel today. Even now that there is an independent internationally recognized State of Israel (since 1948), Jerusalem remains hotly disputed. The Palestinians claim the city as the capital of a Palestinian state; the Muslim world claims it as their third most holy city; the Pope wants to internationalize Jerusalem as a Holy City for Christianity, Judaism, and Islam; and the United Nations have consistently refused to accept Israel's decision after the Six Day War in 1967 to make Jerusalem the undivided capital of the State of Israel.

THE PLACE OF GOD'S CHOICE

What do we know about the historical location of the temple? We know that Solomon built this temple in Jerusalem, on Mount Moriah: *"Then Solomon began to build the temple of the Lord in Jerusalem on Mount Moriah, where the Lord had appeared to his father David. It was on the threshing floor of Araunah the Jebusite, the place provided by David"* (2 Chron. 3:1). This was the same Mount Moriah where Abraham had been prepared to sacrifice Isaac to the Lord; instead, God gave him a ram to sacrifice in Isaac's place (see Gen. 22:1-14; Rom. 8:32). It was the mountain that Abraham had called, *"The Lord Will Provide. And to this day it is said, 'On the mountain of the Lord it will be provided'"* (Gen. 22:14b). Grace characterized the site of the temple. It was not a place where people provided for God's needs (as so

137

many temples of other gods appeared to do). It was the place where God provided for the needs of His people (see 1 Kings 8:31-53).

The site of the temple, Mount Zion, and Mount Moriah are one and the same place. The link between the temple and Mount Zion is particularly clear from First Maccabees 14:26, which states: "They wrote this [an account of the exploits of Simon Maccabeus] on bronze tablets and applied them to the pillars on Mount Zion." Verse 48 reiterates this: "They ordered that this decree should be inscribed on bronze tablets and set up in the Temple precinct in a prominent place."

But why was the temple situated there?

Moses had referred to *"the place the Lord will choose as a dwelling for His Name"* (Deut. 16:2b; see also verses 11,15), making it clear that the location was to be chosen by God. However, much time passed before the Lord made known His choice to King David, as reported by Solomon:

> *Since the day I brought My people Israel out of Egypt, I have not chosen a city in any tribe of Israel to have a temple built for My Name to be there, but I have chosen David to rule My people Israel. My father David had it in his heart to build a temple for the Name of the Lord, the God of Israel. But the Lord said to my father David, "Because it was in your heart to build a temple for My Name, you did well to have this in your heart. Nevertheless, you are not the one to build the temple, but your son, who is your own flesh and blood—he is the one who will build the temple for My name." ... [And now] I have provided a place there for the ark, in which is the covenant of the Lord that He made with our fathers when He brought them out of Egypt* (1 Kings 8:16-19,21; see also 2 Samuel 7-17).

Solomon was responsible for the building, but David had made all the preparations, as he explained to Solomon: *"I have taken great pains to provide for the temple of the Lord a hundred thousand talents of gold, a million talents of silver, quantities of bronze and iron too great to be weighed, and wood and stone. And you may add to them...Now begin the work, and the Lord be with you*" (1 Chron. 22:14,16). David had also identified the site where the temple would be built. God chose the man after His own heart, and David made God's choice. The Lord inspired David's heart and thus David's choice became God's choice.

In Psalm 132, David had said, "*I will allow no sleep to my eyes, no slumber to my eyelids, till I find a place for the Lord, a dwelling for the Mighty One of Jacob*" (Ps. 132:4-5). Jerusalem was to be the city where the Lord chose to establish His name (see 2 Chron. 12:13). The mountain of His inheritance was the place that the Lord had chosen for His dwelling place (see Exod. 15:17; 1 Kings 11:32,36; 14:21). "*For the Lord has chosen Zion, He has desired it for His dwelling: 'This is My resting place for ever and ever; here I will sit enthroned, for I have desired it'*" (Ps. 132:13-14). Psalm 132 clearly shows that the Lord, David and his descendants, Jerusalem, and the mountain (Moriah) are in an insoluble relationship.

David knew that this was to be the place because this was where he had seen the angel that had brought destruction to Israel because of David's sin.

> "*When the angel stretched out his hand to destroy Jerusalem, the Lord was grieved because of the calamity and said to the angel who was afflicting the people, 'Enough! Withdraw your hand!' The angel of the Lord was then at the threshing floor of Araunah the Jebusite*" (2 Samuel 24:16).

Because Mount Zion is not one hill but part of a mountain range, the Lord made it perfectly clear what exact site He had chosen, namely this threshing floor; and the prophet Gad instructed David to erect an altar to the Lord there (see 2 Sam. 24:18).

David could have chosen to seize the threshing floor; instead, he bought it from Araunah (or Ornan) the Jebusite (see 2 Sam. 24:18-25). He paid 50 silver shekels for it, but for the place for the altar, he gave six hundred golden shekels (see 1 Chron. 21:14-25). Only gold was good enough for the Lord, for it is a metal that represents the glory of God. The Lord then confirmed the choice of the site by allowing fire to descend from Heaven: "*David built*

*an altar to the Lord there and sacrificed burnt offerings and fellowship offerings.
He called on the Lord, and the Lord answered him with fire from heaven on the
altar of burnt offering"* (see 1 Chron. 21:26).

Moses had said that God would choose His own place to dwell, and
through His servant David, God chose the city of Jerusalem and Mount Zion.

When the temple built there by King Solomon was being dedicated, *"the
cloud filled the temple of the Lord. And the priests could not perform their service because of the cloud, for the glory of the Lord* [shekhinah] *filled His temple"*
(1 Kings 8:10b-11). The Lord dwelt in the holy of holies in the temple. He
was present in the cloud as He had been present during the earlier wander-
ings in the desert, when the cloud had covered the tabernacle. Exodus
40:34-38 says:

> *Then the cloud covered the Tent of Meeting, and the glory of the Lord
> filled the tabernacle. Moses could not enter the Tent of Meeting be-
> cause the cloud had settled upon it, and the glory of the Lord filled the
> tabernacle. In all the travels of the Israelites, whenever the cloud lifted
> from above the tabernacle, they would set out; but if the cloud did not
> lift, they did not set out—until the day it lifted. So the cloud of the
> Lord was over the tabernacle by day, and fire was in the cloud by
> night, in the sight of all the house of Israel during all their travels.*

Of course, Solomon knew very well that God couldn't be confined to a
temple made of stone. At the dedication, he asked, *"But will God really dwell
on earth? The heavens, even the highest heaven, cannot contain You. How much
less this temple I have built!"* (1 Kings 8:27). Isaiah, too, knew this when he
spoke in God's name, *"…Heaven is My throne and the earth is My footstool…"*
(Isa. 66:1), words that Jesus repeated when He called Heaven the throne of
God, the earth His footstool, and Jerusalem the city of the great King (see
Matt. 5:34-35). And yet the Lord Himself chose Jerusalem as the place on
earth where He would dwell. Again He confirms this place to be His choice
for the second time by fire from Heaven, just as He did on the altar that
King David had built. *"When Solomon finished praying, fire came down from*

heaven and consumed the burnt offering and the sacrifices, and the glory of the
Lord filled the temple" (2 Chron. 7:1).

DESTRUCTION AND RECONSTRUCTION

David prepared. Solomon built. Nebuchadnezzar destroyed (see 2 Chron.
36:19).

After the Babylonian captivity, a second temple was built by Zerubbabel
(see 1 Chron. 3:19; Ezra 2:2; 3:2,8; 4:2-3). Little is known about this temple,
other than that it was built by decree: *"This is what Cyrus king of Persia says:*
'The Lord, the God of heaven, has given me all the kingdoms of the earth and He
has appointed me to build a temple for Him at Jerusalem in Judah'" (Ezra 1:2).
Zerubbabel appears in the genealogy of the Lord Jesus (see Matt. 1:12), and
is mentioned by the prophets Haggai and Zechariah after the Babylonian
exile (see Hag. 1:1-2;12-14; Zech. 4:6-10). Haggai calls him a signet ring of
the Lord (see Hag. 2:23). The temple built by Zerubbabel was much smaller
and less beautiful than that of Solomon (see Ezra 3:12), and there was no ark
in the holy of holies. Therefore, there was no mercy seat where the blood of
the sacrifice could be sprinkled. Jewish tradition records that there was a
stone in it, on which the high priest set incense on the Day of Atonement.
And we never read that the glory of the Lord entered this temple as He did in
Solomon's temple.

Many years later, Herod the Great constructed beautiful additions to
this small temple in an attempt to win favor with the Jewish population.
However, these building activities had barely been completed when the Romans destroyed the temple in A.D. 70. According to some, a small temple,
with rituals and a high priest named Eleazar, was built in A.D. 132 during
the time of Bar Kochba (who led the Jewish revolt against Emperor
Hadrian because he had not kept his promise to rebuild the temple). But in
A.D. 135, Hadrian recaptured Jerusalem, destroyed the Bar Kochba temple,
and set up in its place a Roman temple dedicated to Juno, Jupiter, and Min-
erva. The name of Jerusalem was changed to Aelia Capitolina, and it became a Roman fortress.

Dreams of rebuilding the temple revived under Emperor Julian the Apostate in A.D. 363. Funds and building materials were secured; but on May 19, 363, the day before building operations were to commence, there was a great earthquake. Underground gases exploded and the building materials were destroyed by fire. Hence, the building project collapsed. Hope of rebuilding the temple flared again under Empress Eudocia (married to Emperor Theodosius II, who himself lived in Jerusalem in A.D. 443), but to no avail.

In 614, the Jews assisted the Persians in defeating Heraclius, a Christian Caesar, and were given permission to rebuild the temple. The Persian king, Chosroes II, appointed a Jew by the name of Nehemiah, governor of the city; and history seemed to be about to repeat itself. The walls of Jerusalem had in the past been rebuilt by another Nehemiah, also with the permission of a Persian king (see Neh. 2:1-10)! For a brief period (614-617), the Jews enjoyed the favor of the Persian shah, but later (possibly in response to Christian pressure), he changed his mind and the promised temple was never built. Worse still, the Persians drove the Jews out of Jerusalem; and when Heraclius recaptured Jerusalem 15 years later, all hopes died as he built an octagonal church on the Temple Mount.

In 638, Islamic armies conquered the Holy Land, and between 691 and 692, caliph Abd al-Malik replaced the octagonal Christian church with the octagonal Dome of the Rock, also called the Mosque of Omar, with its gold-covered dome that dominates the Jerusalem skyline. A quotation from the Koran is written on the mosque: "Allah has no Son," which is clearly directed against the Christian world, and against John 3:16, where it is written: *"For God so loved the world that He gave His one and only Son [only begotten Son—KJV], that whoever believes in Him shall not perish but have eternal life."* The Al Aqsa Mosque was built at the other end of the former Temple Square. From this mosque, hatred of the Jewish people is often preached during the Friday services—hatred of those whom the Bible calls God's firstborn son, the apple of His eye. Both mosques stand on the ancient Jewish and Christian holy sites, and for centuries, the idea of a third Jewish temple remained an impossible dream.

Then came June 7, 1967, when Israeli troops under the leadership of Moshe Dayan recaptured the Temple Mount. But on that very same day, he gave orders for the Jewish flag on top of the Dome of the Rock to be lowered; and on June 17, 1967, he placed the Temple Mount in the hands of the Waqf, the Islamic authority—to avoid a Third World War, he said!

The Temple Mount is once again forbidden to Jews. They may not even go there to pray, but must remain below at the Wailing Wall, the Western Wall, a remnant of Herod's temple complex. Nevertheless, Orthodox Jews refuse to go there, in order to avoid the risk of stepping on the place where once was the holy of holies, the most holy place, the innermost part of the temple where the shekhinah glory, the divine presence of the Lord once dwelt.

TEMPLE OF THE ANTICHRIST?

Preparations for the rebuilding of the temple are in full swing in all kinds of Jewish organizations. Assisting in these preparations is the use of a copper scroll, discovered among the Dead Sea Scrolls in the Qumran caves in 1952, which interpreters maintain lists 64 places where temple treasures are hidden or buried. Rabbi Goren insists that temple treasures are hidden deep under the Temple Mount. These treasures might even include the ark of the covenant, hidden since the destruction of the temple by Nebuchadnezzar in 586 B.C..

The Institute of Talmudic Studies has already published more than 25 books about a new temple; and the "temple faithful" regularly try to lay the cornerstone for a new temple, but are hindered by the authorities. A large number of Israelis with the appropriate genealogy are being instructed in priestly duties in yeshivas (Jewish schools of learning); the Temple Institute has woven the prescribed priestly garments; and funds have been earmarked for the building of the temple. When the time comes, the building can be erected quickly. The breeding of the red heifer, whose ashes were used in the ritual purification of persons and objects defiled by a corpse (see Num. 19) and for other purposes in the rituals of the sacrifices in the temple, has started; and some say they have already managed to raise a calf to become a red cow like that one.

Certain expositors maintain that this new temple will be built; they also claim that the Bible teaches that an antichrist will reign for seven years. Shortly after he comes to power, he will stop the ongoing sacrifices, and desecrate this temple.

Is this possibly the temple to which the Lord Jesus referred when He mentioned "the abomination that causes desolation" standing in the holy place (see Matt. 24:15; Dan. 9:27; 11:31; 12:11)? A temple in which sometime during this prophetic "week" (a period of seven years?), a prince, a ruler, will put an end to the revived practice of sacrifice and grain offerings (see Dan. 9:27)? Consent for the building of this temple could be part of a seven-year agreement, a peace treaty, which this "prince" might conclude with Israel. Were such a seven-year pact ever made, the temple could be rebuilt in eight months and the sacrifices resumed. Daniel says:

> Then I heard a holy one speaking, and another holy one said to him, "How long will it take for the vision to be fulfilled—the vision concerning the daily sacrifice, the rebellion that causes desolation, and the surrender of the sanctuary and of the host that will be trampled underfoot?" He said to me, "It will take 2,300 evenings and mornings; then the sanctuary will be reconsecrated" (Daniel 8:13-14).

So, for about six years and four months, this temple will be desecrated. Add eight months for the building of this temple, and your answer is seven years. But this can be the case only if the start of the constructing of this new temple coincides with the rise of an antichrist. Of course, the preparations for the actual building of this temple would take much longer; but even today, people in Israel are already at work.

How might such an agreement with such a world leader come about?

Many scenarios are feasible. It might be the ending to a war that takes place, and the war might be one in which the Islamic world fights, or tries to fight with, Israel. Prophecies still unfulfilled speak of an alliance of all the surrounding nations against Israel (see Ps. 83:1-8), and of the sudden destruction of Damascus (in Syria) (see Isa. 17:1-3). And Egypt will get a blow from tiny Israel as never before, with a positive outcome for Egypt—they will serve YHWH (see Isa. 19)! The prophets also speak of an invasion from the north by Gog (see Ezek. 38–39) (the leader of Russia?) along with the allies mentioned in Ezekiel 38:5-6, who might be identified as Iran, Afghanistan, Libya, Turkey, Ethiopia, Sudan, and Iraq. Syria, Egypt, and Jordan (Edom—see Ezekiel 35 and 36!) are not mentioned in the list, so it might be that a devastating battle will have already taken place. Whatever the details of the case, the final peace agreement might include the rebuilding of the Jewish temple as a real possibility.

Where might this new temple be built? Could it be between the two mosques on the Temple Mount, as a symbol of the brotherhood of religions? Will it have the approval of the Christian world? Could the Temple Mount and the Islamic, Christian, and Jewish holy places in Jerusalem be placed under an "International Religious Committee" installed by the United Nations and placed under the rotating chairmanship of a Jew, a Muslim, and a Christian? Anything is feasible. One can imagine many possible scenarios. An earthquake might do the trick, or bombs dropped on the mosques in a future war in the Middle East, or whatever.

In any case, Paul says that the antichrist will reveal himself in a temple and claim to be a god (see 2 Thess. 2:4). The final revelation of satan is in this man of perdition, the antichrist, who will set himself upon the throne of God in the temple. It is impossible to imagine a greater abomination in the holy place. John says that the outer court of the temple will be trodden under foot by the Gentiles (see Rev. 11:2) for 42 months. But John also refers to this temple in Revelation chapter 11 as a temple of God in which true prayer takes place (see Rev. 11:1). Jesus, Paul, and John all speak about a temple. Do they mean a literal temple? Do they mean the Church? Jews hope and pray for the rebuilding of the temple in order to revive the heart of the Jewish religion. But it might well be that if such a temple were to be built, it would be quickly desecrated by the man of sin, a man who wants to be god. That was the temptation presented by satan in the first book of the Bible. "You will be like God," he said, "when you disobey God's instructions."

The final question is whether the evidence offered above is sufficient to necessitate the rebuilding of the temple in Jerusalem before Jesus returns. Can the texts of Jesus' discourse about the last days, the letters of Paul, and John's Revelation of Jesus Christ be spiritually interpreted? Is it possible that the concept of a temple, refers to the Church, a Christendom governed by antichristian thinking, like the "goddess of reason" who was worshipped in Notre Dame cathedral in Paris during the French Revolution? It certainly is possible. It is necessary to examine these passages for spiritual lessons too. But such lessons do not preclude a literal rebuilding of the temple. So many prophecies have already been fulfilled literally since Israel's restoration to the Promised Land that such a thing should not surprise us at all, regardless of the problems it poses for Christian theology.

Moreover, realizing that this new temple, which might be built in Jerusalem, will quickly be defiled, also offers us a personal spiritual lesson. We, too, need to be on the alert lest our bodies, which are the temples of the Holy Spirit, be desecrated by excessive alcohol, drugs, gluttony and obesity, or by exhausting ourselves through a lack of proper rest, excessive stress, bitterness, or other sins of the flesh.

And the church organization, which is our spiritual home, can also be filled with antichristian theology and philosophies that center on fallen man. We all are called to be watchmen on the walls—both on the walls of the earthly Jerusalem, and on the walls of the Church. Like Ezra, Nehemiah, and their men, when they were rebuilding the city of Jerusalem and the temple, we need to keep watch both in prayer and by concrete action.

Is there a spiritual lesson here for the Christian Church, even before these prophetic words are literally fulfilled? Sometimes in the New Testament, the

Church is called a temple, or a spiritual house, or a body. Is not the rise of humanistic theology in the Church, whereby everything revolves around man considering to be a god himself in the depth of his inner being, a kind of fulfillment of these prophecies? Man, who thinks that because of the divine spark within, he is like god, and therefore wants to decide for himself about good and evil without recourse to any outside authority. Does that not sound like a fulfillment of these prophecies? Is the Church already engaged in a kind of idolatry—worshiping man, rather than God? Where that is the case, she will end up part of the false church of the endtime.

Another possible interpretation of the passage in Matthew 24:15 is that we might not have to wait for a literal temple to be rebuilt in Jerusalem and then defiled by a historic figure, the antichrist. Maybe the "abomination that causes desolation" is already there. Islam rules in the holy place. (Jesus did not use the word "temple" but spoke of the "holy place," which could well be Mount Zion itself.) Hatred and violence against the Jews (and Christians) are preached in the Islamic mosques on Mount Zion—hatred and violence that could eventually lead to more and more destruction. Hatred that might lead one day to a *jihad* (holy war) against Israel, a war so powerful and destructive that Jesus, in His eschatological preaching on the Mount of Olives, advised the Jews to flee (see Matt. 24).

NEARER TO THE RETURN

The desecration of a possible third temple will cease when the Messiah Himself (Jesus Christ) finally appears. Then the holy place will be properly restored (see Dan. 8:14). Sometimes I think, *The more people talk about the rebuilding of the temple, the closer we come to the return of Christ.*

Will this third temple lead to a fourth temple, like the first temple of Solomon was followed by the second temple of Zerubbabel, which was enlarged and embellished by Herod the Great (so much so that Herod's structure is sometimes called the third temple)? That seems not to be the case. Ezekiel chapters 40 to 48 describe a temple complex that will exist after Gog and his allies are defeated on the mountains of Israel; their defeat is described in chapters

38 and 39. This third temple of the antichrist—if at all—apparently exists only briefly and will probably be destroyed in the final battle and earthquakes around Jerusalem. If it is ever built, it will be merely an interim temple—a Jewish dream that will eventually go up in smoke.

All expositors agree that this temple has not yet been built. But in my opinion, one day, there will be another temple in Jerusalem. Ezekiel chapters 40 to 48 speak clearly about that temple; and the glory of the Lord will again enter into that temple (see Ezek. 43).

The temple of Ezekiel, which will be the final temple, seems to be located in a different place—not on the Temple Mount in Jerusalem, but far outside the actual city. Zechariah says that Jerusalem will continue to be in its own place (see Zech. 12:6); the area to the south will become a plain (see Zech. 14:10), while the mountain of the house of the Lord will be established as the chief of the mountains and will be raised above the hills (see Isa. 2:2).

These details mean that the geography in and around Jerusalem will probably change. The Mount of Olives will split in two (see Zech. 14:4). Jerusalem will be hit by an earthquake (see Rev. 11:13), but in the end it will be an open place (see Zech. 2:4-5). No protective walls of any sort will be needed because there will be peace. The Prince of Peace will be there. No matter how dark history might yet become for the world and for the Middle East, Israel is on the way to her rest. He will come to give her rest. And the Lord will have His resting-place there forever (see Ps. 132:14).

Just as Israel is on the way to her rest centered on an earthly Jerusalem, so the Church is on her way to rest in the heavenly Jerusalem (see Heb. 12:22-24). But one day that heavenly Jerusalem will descend to earth, when a new Heaven and a new earth are formed, where righteousness will dwell (see 2 Pet. 3:13; Rev. 21–22:5). One can only speculate about the relationship between the two Jerusalems in the Messianic Kingdom of peace (see Rev. 20:1-10; Zech. 14:8-21). After Jesus' resurrection, He appeared for 40 days to His disciples before He went to Heaven. He probably moved back and forth between our earthly dimension and the heavenly realm. Perhaps this will also be the case when we are living with Him in resurrection life during the Millennium (see Rev. 20:4-6).

What we can be sure of is that ultimately, God will be all and in all (see 1 Cor. 15:28). Maranatha! Come Lord Jesus (see Rev. 22:20; 1 Cor. 16:22)!

CHAPTER ELEVEN

Your Kingdom Come

When the Lord Jesus taught His disciples the beautiful prayer known as the Lord's Prayer, He began: "*Our Father in heaven, hallowed be Your name, Your kingdom come, Your will be done, on earth as it is in heaven*" (Matt. 6:9-10; see also verse 11-14).

What did He mean by praying for the "kingdom to come"? Are we praying for a spiritual kingdom in people's hearts? That certainly is part of it. Paul said, "*For the kingdom of God is not a matter of eating and drinking, but of righteousness, peace and joy in the Holy Spirit*" (Rom. 14:17). By being born again, a person receives the Holy Spirit—"*Having believed, you were marked in Him with a seal, the promised Holy Spirit*" (Eph. 1:13b). And thus, the Church is one form of the Kingdom of God, a community of people who through faith in Christ and the indwelling of the Holy Spirit serve Christ in the world. By words and deeds, they help to establish signs of the Kingdom that is to come, just as He Himself did during His lifetime. He referred to His own miracles as "signs of the Kingdom" for they were bright spots in the darkness, examples and indicators pointing to the Kingdom yet to come. The sick were healed, the dead raised, the hungry fed, the blind received their eyesight, and the deaf their hearing…and, yes, sins were forgiven.

When John the Baptist, who had been imprisoned by Herod, began to doubt whether Jesus was really the Messiah Israel was expecting, he sent his disciples to Jesus with the following question: *"Are you the one who was to come, or should we expect someone else?"* (Matt. 11:3; see also verses 4-6). The answer that Jesus sent back is a direct quotation from Isaiah (see Isa. 29:18-19; 35:5-6; 61:1-2). If you look up Isaiah 35, you will see that the quotation slips over into the prophetic vision of a renewed creation.

> *Then will the eyes of the blind be opened and the ears of the deaf un-stopped. Then will the lame leap like a deer, and the mute tongue shout for joy. Water will gush forth in the wilderness and streams in the desert. The burning sand will become a pool, the thirsty ground bubbling springs. In the haunts where jackals once lay, grass and reeds and papyrus will grow* (Isaiah 35:5-7).

But immediately before saying this, Isaiah had said: *"Be strong, do not fear; your God will come, He will come with vengeance; with divine retribution He will come to save you"* (Isa. 35:4b). What John was really asking was: "Are You the King, the Messiah, who will bring judgment to the godless and then establish the Kingdom of peace?" Jesus did not deny it.

THREE PHASES OF THE KINGDOM

What is the Kingdom of God? Where is the Kingdom of God? And how is the Kingdom of God? Basically, wherever God (through Jesus) is in authority, the Kingdom is present. So when Jesus was in person on earth, the first phase of the Kingdom was present. When Jesus went to Heaven, He told His disciples that through the Holy Spirit in them, He would show the same signs of the Kingdom as He had showed them on earth through them. So the second phase of the Kingdom is the phase of the Church, the invisible Kingdom in the hearts of men. And the third phase of the Kingdom will begin when Jesus returns to earth and establishes His Kingdom worldwide.

Jesus answered a question about when the Kingdom of God would come by saying, *"The kingdom of God does not come with your careful observation* [its date cannot be calculated using some formula], *nor will people say, 'Here it is,' or 'There it is,' because the kingdom of God is within you"* (Luke 17:20b-21). "Within you" can also be translated as "among you." Both translations are correct, for both meanings are true. Wherever Jesus is, the Kingdom is; and the signs of the Kingdom will be present. Consider all the miracles that occurred during His lifetime. The Kingdom was really present, because He was there in person. This Scripture also means that when Jesus is in you by His Holy Spirit, the Kingdom is also present in you. Hence, He says that signs and miracles will also accompany believers (see Mark 16:17-18), to such an extent that they will do even greater things than He has done (see John 14:12)!

Although the Kingdom of God came very near with Christ's first coming to Israel—the first phase of the Kingdom—that was not yet the time for it to fill the earth. It is worth taking a close look at the incident in the synagogue when He read from Isaiah 61 and announced His ministry. Luke reports it as follows:

> *"The Spirit of the Lord is on Me, because He has anointed Me to preach good news to the poor. He has sent Me to proclaim freedom for the prisoners and recovery of sight for the blind, to release the oppressed, to proclaim the year of the Lord's favor." Then He rolled up the scroll, gave it back to the attendant and sat down…*[Then He announced], *"Today this scripture is fulfilled in your hearing"* (Luke 4:18-21).

But when you look at this passage in Isaiah 61, it includes a few more words that Jesus did not read: "[to proclaim] *the day of vengeance of our God!"* (Isa. 61:2). Jesus knew that we had not yet reached that stage. The judgment day, the day of vengeance, that will precede the coming of the Kingdom on earth, was still in the future. Before it came, there was to be the year of the Lord's favor. That favorable year in which the Gospel can be proclaimed worldwide has already lasted for nearly two thousand years. People everywhere can come to the Lord, have their sins forgiven, and be permitted to experience one form of the Kingdom—Jesus in their heart. There is to be a long period of grace before the Day of the Lord comes. These elements were woven together in the Old Testament prophecies, and the strands were unravelled by the Lord Jesus.

First the presence of Jesus Himself; then the spreading of the Gospel worldwide; then the judgment of the Kingdom. First the hidden form of the Kingdom in the hearts of the people; then the Kingdom in its outward, visible worldwide form. And that visible Kingdom will be inseparably bound to Israel.

After the Lord Jesus had completed His work on the cross and given His precious blood for the sins (plural) of the world; after He had broken the power of sin (singular), defeating the devil and his powers of darkness; after His triumphant resurrection, and immediately before His ascension, His disciples excitedly asked:

> *"Lord, are You at this time going to restore the kingdom to Israel?"* [The Lord Jesus did not answer, "What a dumb question! Do you still not understand that it is not about an earthly kingdom in which Israel will have a prominent place, but that it is all about a heavenly, spiritual kingdom?" No. All He said was:] *"It is not for you to know the times or dates the Father has set by His own authority. But you will receive power when the Holy Spirit comes on you; and you will be My witnesses in Jerusalem, and in all Judea and Samaria, and to the ends of the earth"* (Acts 1:6-8).

These were His last words before the enveloping cloud of God's (shekhinah) glory took Him away (see Luke 9:34-35).

He spoke of the same things in His discourse on the Mount of Olives regarding final events and the end of this age: *"And this gospel of the kingdom will be preached in the whole world as a testimony to all nations, and then the end will come"* (Matt. 24:14). The hidden form of the Kingdom in the hearts of people, in the Church of Jesus Christ, must come first.

THE KINGDOM IS LIFE

It is worth noting that the proclamation of the Gospel of the Kingdom is not the preaching of a revolution. If Jesus had intended to establish a kingdom by force, He would never have said to Pilate, *"My kingdom is not of this world."* In Greek, the word is *aioon/aeon*, meaning, "this world period, this phase through which world history is passing, this age." What Jesus said was, *"My kingdom is not of this world* [this age, this aeon]. *If it were, My servants would fight to prevent My arrest by the Jews. But now My kingdom is from another place"* (John 18:36).

Yet when Pilate then asked Him if He really was a king, Jesus confirmed it.

But He is more than merely a king; He is also the way, the truth, and the life. He is the way to God. He is the truth against all lies (and against the father of lies, the devil). He is the life—eternal life. He does not merely propagate a theology, a philosophy, or a theory; He is what He preaches! He Himself, in person, is it!

The first thing Jesus had to do was to conquer the death principle that had ruled all of creation since the fall, when God had stated: *"Cursed is the ground because of you…"* (Gen. 3:17b). Sin led to both humans and the rest of creation experiencing death. Paul reminds us:

> *For the creation was subjected to frustration, not by its own choice, but by the will of the one who subjected it, in hope that the creation itself will be liberated from its bondage to decay and brought into the glorious freedom of the children of God. We know that the whole creation has been groaning as in the pains of childbirth right up to the present time* (Romans 8:20-22).

Creation is not in a process of evolving upwards; it is in a downward spiral toward death and extinction. A principle of death rules creation, as a result of the sin of man. We can hardly imagine what creation would have been like had we obeyed God. Even today, if people would listen to God's Word, the Bible, which contains His directions for life, earth would be a much better place, despite sin. The magnificent natural world is suffering because of us. And still, we are polluting the earth, robbing it of its natural resources, leaving nothing for our children and grandchildren. May the Kingdom and the renewal of all things come soon!

PRELUDE TO DELIVERANCE

The turning point in history has passed. Christ has died, and what is more, He has risen from the dead! The bridgehead of the victory is secured. From this point on, everything will be different. First, He will establish His Kingdom in the hearts and minds of the people of His Church, through the Holy Spirit. After that, when He comes in glory for all to see, His Kingdom will be openly and visibly established. Israel has everything to do with this. The return of the Jewish people, as we have seen it take place before our very eyes during the past few decades, has everything to do with this. It is the beginning, the prelude, to worldwide deliverance. Israel is on the way to her rest. The law will go out from Jerusalem (see Isa. 2:2-4), and people will learn war no more (see Mic. 4:3). Peace will cover the whole earth. Then the Kingdom will have come, because the King of that Kingdom has come, the Messiah of Israel, the King of kings, and the Lord of lords—Jesus Christ (see Rev. 19:11-16).

Will the history of this world simply flow on into this Kingdom? Will the return of Christ round off and complete the peace process that mankind is trying to set up (and which is occupying so much of the time and minds of the people who are preaching a new world order)? Will it be the capstone on a human structure? No. That capstone will be the antichrist, the christ-in-the-place-of-Christ. The Greek word *anti* means "in the place of," but it can also mean "against." He will be against Christ, against God, against the Christians and the Jews, against the Bible. Beautiful theories and slogans will be touted, using words like *freedom, justice, reconciliation, tolerance, unity of all religions, peace, wealth, bread, and fun for all.* Promises will be made; the state will guarantee prosperity, fortune, and happiness for all. There will be free medicine and medical care for everyone. There will be no boundaries or limits. Science will guarantee our future and will overcome all our problems. Sexual lusts will be satisfied as never before.

People who oppose these glorious developments will be judged to be in need of reeducation or retraining. If they persist in their objections, they will be sent to psychiatric hospitals (as in the former USSR) or annihilated in concentration camps. It will be known how to locate these people, because our administrative systems will be flawless. Our computers will be all-powerful. And our police forces, both national and international, will be meticulous. Everyone will be forced to toe the line, for their own good, and for the good of all. The beast will insist that everyone worship him, and everyone will worship him (see Rev. 13:8). Whoever does not, will be an outcast—shut out of the economy, and finally persecuted and killed (see Rev. 13)!

Those who stay true to Christ and the Word of God will pay with their lives (see Rev. 6:11). The woman, the whore, will be drunk with the blood of the saints (see Rev. 17:6). *"But he who stands firm to the end will be saved"* (Matt. 24:13). Time and again, history has shown what happens when people try to establish the kingdom on their own. "Liberty, equality, fraternity" was the slogan of the French Revolution; but streams of blood flowed, and the revolution devoured her own children. The communist revolution advocated by Karl Marx was supposed to lead inevitably to a utopian classless society. The upshot was tens of millions of casualties in Russia and China, and a totally impoverished and disintegrating society. Hitler intended to build a Third Reich, a kingdom of peace—yet never has Europe, and ultimately the whole world, gone through such a dark night. Many people lost their lives, while the main thrust of hate was directed toward the Jews and the Christians, the people of the Book. Interestingly, the hatred was not also directed at Muslims, even though some people consider them to be people of the Book as well. On the contrary, the Arab world stood right behind Germany and hoped Hitler would succeed with his *Endlösung*, the killing of all Jews in the world.

The truth is—the Kingdom, the Kingdom of peace, will come only when Christ returns.

That happy event will be preceded by God's worldwide catastrophic and apocalyptic judgments, which the great visionary John describes in the Book of Revelation. When the demonic powers seem to have almost full control and seem to be ruling the entire world, then He will come and make all things new. He will bring to fulfillment all the promises made to His people Israel, as well as all the promises He has made to His Church.

A form of reformed theology (endorsed by Abraham Kuyper) once taught that the Gospel would be spread all over the world so that the whole world would become Christianized. "The Kingdom is for the worldwide Church," they said. Then Christ would return, as the capstone of the preaching of the Gospel. Judgment would follow, and the new Heaven and earth would arrive.

The Roman Catholic Church taught that the Church possessed two swords—a spiritual one and a temporal (worldly) one. The Church herself handled the spiritual sword, while the temporal sword was handled by the state and by worldly rulers who would follow the Church's instructions. There was no role for Israel. A kingdom with Israel at its center was inconceivable.

But the exact opposite of what was expected is now happening. Christianity is collapsing in the Western world, but Israel is coming home. The Gospel is still being preached to the ends of the earth, and rich blessings are following. But persecution is setting in as well. And although every Christian will and must do his utmost for God, it will not bring the final Kingdom. The most that can happen is that signs of that Kingdom will be seen.

It is possible that there is even a relationship between the fact that synagogues are being closed all over the world because the Jews are returning to Israel and the fact that Christianity is declining. This is particularly so in Europe, where we have murdered and literally wiped out whole Jewish communities and their synagogues. Maybe there is and always has been a spiritual relationship between the synagogue and the Church that we as Christians have never seen or realized. The synagogue did not (and could not, because of Christian theology) see that spiritual relationship, and the Church undoubtedly has not seen it.

However, consider that Paul said we are grafted onto the old root. Yet the Church has cut that root. During Church history, the Church first cut the root theologically, and then it cut the Jewish root literally by encouraging the persecution of the Jews. The Nazis, for instance, could quote Luther, who said the most terrible things about the Jews. During the time of the Inquisition, Jews were burned at the stake with crucifixes held before their eyes. The Russian Orthodox Church encouraged pogroms, especially during the Holy Week before Easter. And so forth. We cut the root and stole the fruit. But when you cut the root, whatever is grafted onto that root will also wither and eventually die. And Christianity is dying, especially in Europe.

One thing is certain—the Church is not going to bring in the Kingdom. And another thing is certain as well—God *will* bring in the Kingdom! Christ will bring the Kingdom, and perhaps very soon! The return of the Jews to their own land of Israel in our day tells us that Jesus is coming. Who knows how soon that will be. Maranatha!

CHAPTER TWELVE

Peace

ZIONISM

In August 1997, the World Jewish Congress in Basel, Switzerland, cel-ebrated the 100th anniversary of the first Zionist Congress held there under the leadership of Theodor Herzl. Zionism was and is the Jewish movement with only one goal—home. Home to Israel. Home to Zion. It was felt that the centuries-long dispersion all over the world must come to an end, and there must be an independent Jewish State. But where should that be? That was not immediately clear. Some even suggested that land somewhere in Africa might be acquired as a homeland for the Jews. But God had other plans.

GOING HOME

Of course, the homeland had to be Israel. And Jews began to arrive, flee-ing the pogroms in Russia at the end of the 20th century. At first, they came predominantly from the lands of central Europe, Poland, and the Balkans.

In 1897, Herzl had foretold that within 50 years there would be a Jewish State of Israel, and exactly 50 years later, his prophecy came true. Ezekiel prophesied about the return of the dispersed Jews, when he saw the valley of the dry bones come to life and the bones come together with muscles, flesh, and skin to cover them; and he was permitted to breathe life into them. In explanation of the vision, the Lord said: *"O My people, I am going to open your graves and bring you up from them* [out of the 'graves' of the nations, in which Israel almost seemed to have disappeared]; *I will bring you back to the land of Israel"* (Ezek. 37:12b).

In 1947, the General Assembly of the United Nations decided that the Jews should have their own homeland in Palestine, as it was then called. But nowhere in the Bible is the land of Canaan called Palestine. That name was derived from the name of the Philistines, the archenemies of Israel in the Old Testament. The Romans also called the area Palestine, as do the United Nations.

Nonetheless, the land of Israel—that is her name. That is what the angel called it in Joseph's dream (Luke 2:20-21); and that is where the Jews are destined to go. We have seen it happening before our very eyes for more than one hundred years, even as they staggered out of the concentration camps of Western Europe, living skeletons on their way home.

The British tried to hold them back, but to no avail. For God's time had arrived. In 1948, the Jewish State was called into being, and in 1998 it celebrated the 50th anniversary of its birth. In the interim, a third 50-year "jubilee" had passed—the 50th anniversary of the Balfour Declaration, in which the British government recognized the right of the Jews to have their own homeland in Palestine. That declaration was issued in 1917; and in 1967, exactly 50 years later, Jerusalem became the undivided capital of the independent State of Israel. The temporary occupation of East Jerusalem by Jordan was over. A land, a people, a city, and a State—God's promises were being fulfilled.

From all over the world they came in great waves, as when, after the collapse of communism in Russia, hundreds of thousands arrived at once, so that today there are more than one million Jews who have emigrated from the former USSR. They have also arrived in small groups, by plane from Arab countries, and from Ethiopia in daring Israeli operations. By sea, by air, even on foot, they have come to the land of Israel. "O Lord, restore us to Zion," they had prayed for many centuries. And now it has really happened. The dream of Zionism has become a reality.

HELP ALONG THE WAY

Among those helping the Jews to return are Christian organizations, such as Christians for Israel International, a growing international and non-political movement of Christians from all churches and denominations who believe that the return of the Jewish people to Israel is a fulfillment of biblical prophecy. We believe that our love and concern for Israel should extend beyond talk; we also want to do something for Israel. If you want to know more about our worldwide organization, please see our web site: www.c4israel.org, or contact us by email through: international@c4 israel.org, or by phone: +31-33-24 588 24.

One of our projects is to help Jews return home to Israel and then assist them at home in Israel. In particular, we have focused on helping some of the estimated one million Jews still living in the former Soviet Union, such as in the Ukraine, a former Soviet republic. That region has experienced an appalling history of anti-Semitism, including several mass murders of Jews, often occurring with the complicity of the church. A painting of the massacre at Babi Yar, a ravine on the outskirts of Kiev, where on September 29-30, 1941, 33,771 Jews were machine-gunned by a special SS unit supported by Ukrainian militia men, is hanging today in the Knesset in Jerusalem. At the end of 778 days of Nazi rule in Kiev, the ravine had become a mass grave for over 100,000 persons, the majority of them being Jews. It has become a symbol for Jewish martyrdom at the hands of the Nazis in the Soviet Union.

"The days are coming," declares the Lord, "when men will no longer say, 'As surely as the Lord lives, who brought the Israelites up out of Egypt,' [the Exodus out of Egypt under the leadership of Moses] *but they will say, 'As surely as the Lord lives, who brought the Israelites*

up out of the land of the north [Babylon and Iraq, but also countries further to the north, such as Russia and the former Soviet Republics] *and out of all the countries where He had banished them.' For I will restore them to the land I gave their forefathers. But now I will send for many fishermen,"* declares the Lord [fishermen try to entice with bait and will gently try to "catch" the Jews, so that they will perceive that it is time to go to Israel of their own free will], *"and they will catch them. After that I will send for many hunters, and they will hunt them down on every mountain and hill and from the crevices of the rocks"* (Jeremiah 16:14-16).

Hunters are there to kill. They will pursue the Jews wherever they can, and only very few will be able to escape. Hitler was such a hunter. Anti-Semitism all over the world is a kind of hunting. There are people like Hitler and many others who will pursue the Jews and kill them as prey, even today.

"Go home," say the fishermen, which include some young Christian volunteers who work in the former USSR on behalf of Christians for Israel International and Ebenezer Emergency Fund, showing the Jews the prophecies in the Bible about the promised return of the Jewish people to their own land, "before the hunters come." Convinced by these arguments, many Jews are ultimately willing to leave their sometimes comfortable homes all over the world, and start to make "aliyah," return to Israel. Thousands are already on their way, helped by Christians worldwide, on an ongoing basis.

BROUGHT HOME BY THE LORD

But who is really bringing the Jews home? Is it Zionism? Is it the actions of Christians for Israel International or the political decisions of the United Nations? Or are they being driven home by the anti-Semitism of people like Hitler and others in the 20th and 21st centuries? Are they driving the Jews home? Yes, it is all of that. But there is more to it. First and foremost, we must make it clear that it is ultimately the Lord who is bringing the Jews home. Through the prophet Isaiah, He tells Israel:

"Do not be afraid, for I am with you; I will bring your children from the east and gather you from the west. I will say to the north, 'Give them up!' and to the south, 'Do not hold them back.' Bring My sons from afar and My daughters from the ends of the earth—everyone who is called by My name, whom I created for My glory, whom I formed and made." Lead out those who have eyes but are blind, who have ears but are deaf (Isaiah 43:5-8).

The Lord is bringing the Jews home. His hand is behind all these human, political, charitable, and ideological acts; it is really by His power that the Jewish people are returning home to Israel. But how does He do it? The Eternal always acts through His Word. Through the Word—the eternal Torah, as the Jews say—creation came into being; and through the Word, creation is upheld until this very day. All that the Lord does is mediated by the Word and by the Ruach YHWH, the Spirit of God. The way of the Lord into the world runs via the Word and the Spirit, and so does the way back from this world to God the Father. *"The Word became flesh and made His dwelling among us"* (John 1:14).

After His crucifixion and resurrection, when He was about to go and sit at the right hand of God, Jesus said, *"All authority in heaven and on earth has been given to Me"* (Matt. 28:18b). He is the Lamb, who is allowed to take the scroll from the right hand of Him who sits upon the throne, to bring world history to a final close (see Rev. 5:1-10), and to bring in the Kingdom of God, even after and through final ordeals, plagues, judgments, and disasters, as the Book of Revelation explains.

The Lord God is bringing the Jews home. And through whom is He bringing them home? Through the Lord Jesus Christ, who sits all-powerful on the throne, at the right hand of the Father. Jesus is bringing the Jews home, even though Israel does not (yet) realize it. Isaiah had prophesied this when he spoke of the Servant of the Lord, being a covenant for the people (Israel) to restore the land and rebuild its ruined cities (see Isa. 49:8). The Servant will be able to say to the prisoners (in the worldwide prisons, concentration camps, and ghettos, scattered among the nations): "Come and appear! Come out! Go! Out of the deep darkness of the graves in which you were buried" (see Isa. 49:9). Who is this Servant of the Lord? Isaiah says that the Lord had formed Him as His Servant from His mother's womb (see Isa. 49:1) (conceived by the Holy Spirit in the womb of His mother Mary). To do what? *"To bring Jacob back to Him and gather Israel to Himself."* Then he adds, *"It is too small a thing for you to be My servant to restore the tribes of Jacob* [the servant is therefore not Israel itself] *and bring back those* [the rest] *of Israel I have kept. I will also make you a light for the Gentiles, that you may bring My salvation to the ends of the earth"* (see Isa. 49:5b-6).

These were the words that Simeon recalled in the temple when he held the infant Jesus in his arms; but in a remarkable twist, Simeon reversed the order! Led by the Holy Spirit, he said, *"Sovereign Lord, as You have promised, You now dismiss Your servant in peace. For my eyes have seen Your salvation, which You have prepared in the sight of all people, a light for revelation to the Gentiles* [that first] *and for glory to Your people Israel* [that next] *"* (Luke 2:29-32).

Israel is on the way to her rest—on the way to glory. The Servant of the Lord in Isaiah, Jesus, is bringing the Jews home. Why? Because He wants to meet them there, in Israel, in Jerusalem, when He will come in glory. The Lord God has given His Son the power to direct history in such a way that Israel returns home; and presently, He will reveal Himself to His Jewish brothers and sisters by the Holy Spirit (see Zech. 12:10-14; 14:4), just as Joseph revealed himself to his brothers in Egypt (see Gen. 45:1-3a). The coming of the Lord is rapidly approaching.

> *This is what the Sovereign Lord says: "See, I will beckon to the Gentiles, I will lift up My banner to the peoples; they will bring your sons in their arms and carry your daughters on their shoulders. Kings will be your foster fathers, and their queens your nursing mothers. They will bow down before you with their faces to the ground"* (Isaiah 49:22-23a).

Israel is on the way to her rest and her glory, and is being brought home by the non-Jews, the Gentiles. By you and me! By believing and non-believing

Gentiles! So, put an arm around a Jewish man, a Jewish woman, a Jewish child, and help them go home! By the busload! And the planeload! The Lord is bringing the Jews home, and He is using the Gentiles to do it. He has initiated the last phase of this age of world history! Immediately after all the darkness and trials (which will certainly increase more and more in the future), His Kingdom will break forth, and the King of that Kingdom, Jesus Christ, the Messiah of Israel, will come in glory. Bring the Jews home, because Jesus, the Messiah of Israel, is coming! Help them travel to the land and help them in the land, until Jesus comes to make all things forever new.

SIGNS OF THE ENDTIME

First, there will be salvation to the Gentiles, followed by glory for the people of Israel. We are nearly there! Salvation, the preaching of the Gospel, is going out into all the nations, and Israel is beginning to return home.

In His last great discourse on the Mount of Olives, the Lord Jesus named signs that would point to the time of His return (see Matt. 24; Luke 21; Mark 13). Many of these signs, such as earthquakes, wars, plagues, hunger, lawlessness, and persecutions have been around on a lesser scale for centuries. But in our day, there has been a spectacular increase in them. More people have died in wars in the 20th century than in all the previous centuries together. False prophets in our century have created more casualties than ever before. Hitler's National Socialism cost six million Jews their lives in the Second World War, as well as the lives of tens of millions of others. Stalin's communism took millions of more lives of Christians and Jews, as did Mao Tse-tung's terror, not to mention what has happened in Cambodia and Rwanda. Moreover, the number of killer quakes (earthquakes that claim many lives) has rapidly increased; and AIDS, cancer, and other sicknesses are claiming ever more victims.

But besides these negative signs, there are two other positive signs that point to the coming of the Messiah, which have not appeared in history—before now. The first of these is the worldwide preaching of the Gospel to all nations (see Matt. 24:14), which is taking place in our day. The 19th century was the great missionary century; and in the 20th and 21st centuries, modern means of communication, such as radio, TV and the Internet are broadcasting the Gospel all over the world. Jesus did not predict that each and every individual would hear the Gospel; what He did say, however, was that every nation would be allowed to hear the Gospel, and then the end would come.

The second sign is the "blossoming of the fig tree," referring to Israel (see Matt. 24:32-33; Joel 1:7). When your eyes see this happening, you need to know that Christ's coming is very near, at your very door (see Matt. 24:33). The Kingdom of God is near (see Luke 21:31). And we are the generation seeing both signs coming to pass, as well as the increase of all the other signs.

PEACE

How will Israel come to her rest? Will it be through the "peace process" in the Middle East, under the leadership of America, Russia, Europe, and the United Nations—the "Quartet"? No. In fact, it is to be feared that when those kind of peace negotiations show signs of succeeding, the greatest misery is about to begin.

False prophets say, "Peace, peace," but there is no peace (see Jer. 6:14; 8:11,15; Ezek. 13:1-16). The antichrist will make a covenant, a peace treaty, with Israel, but will break it in a short time; and as has been predicted, battles and destruction will continue to the very end (see Dan. 9:26b-27; 11:31; Matt. 24:15-22; Mark 13:14-20). When Israel expects to live in peace, suddenly, like an unexpected thunderstorm, enemies will attack (see Ezek. 38:1-16). There will be a kind of peace…and who does not wish that for the Jewish people, who for centuries have been so tried? The Jews really want peace and are willing to take enormous risks by leaving parts of the Promised Land. They are a people who have been bleeding and still are bleeding from many wounds. They desperately want peace. But the nations will come after Jerusalem, the Bible says. All nations will try to lift the immovable rock of Jerusalem, but in the process will suffer severe injury (see Zech. 12:3) in a terrible defeat. Moreover, Israel will spend seven months burying the dead (see Ezek. 38–39). Peace, for which we all hunger, will come only when the God of peace has achieved His goal for His Church and for Israel, and ultimately His goal for the nations and even for creation itself.

Does this mean that we should cease our efforts to promote the peace process in the Middle East and in the world? Certainly not! Peace is better than war, just as having food is better than being hungry. Health is better than sickness; a clean environment is better than a contaminated world; right is better than wrong…but not at all costs. And we must remember what God says in His Word about Israel and the land He has promised to them.

Again and again, it appears that the human heart is cunning and always, in the first place, selfish. It is always inclined to hate God and its neighbor. We think we know better than God does (see Titus 3:3; John 15:25; Rom. 1:28-32; Ps. 143:2; Rom. 3:11). Sin reigns in human hearts. And the powers of darkness are led by the *prince of this world* (see John 14:30; Matt. 4:8-9). Satan reigns over sinful human beings and over the governing bodies—dictators, kings, presidents, democratic governments, in short, the world rulers of this darkness (see Eph. 6:12). In the past, God judged the world with a flood because every inclination of the human heart was to do evil all the time (see Gen. 6:5-8). And when the measure of human evil is once again full, and God's patience is at an end, there will be another worldwide judgment (see 2 Pet. 3:1-13), with destruction by fire.

Great watchfulness is the order of the day, for all peace is temporary and constantly under threat. There is no room for carelessness. We can never let our alertness flag, whether the issues are small or great. Israel should be aware of this too. Even if the Lord does grant a short respite and rest, we need to grasp that this is not yet the end. We are on the way to the Kingdom and to the King of that Kingdom. Not until the last jot and tittle of God's Word has been fulfilled will there be peace (see Matt. 24:35). True peace will emerge only when the Lord Himself has achieved His goal for Israel, when their eyes are opened to Him, and when the Prince of Peace has returned to Jerusalem.

SHOWING FRUITS OF REPENTANCE TO THE JEWS

"Comfort, comfort My people, says your God" (Isa. 40:1). "Arouse them to envy," says Paul (see Rom. 11:14). An important part of being able to do this is an attitude of humility and of admission of guilt. We need to confess our guilt for the attitude of the Church throughout the centuries, when Jews who were hungry, thirsty, strangers among us, naked, sick, and in prison (concentration camps) were not supported. We ignored what the Lord meant when He pointed to those around Him, to each *"one of the least of these brothers of Mine."*

This passage in Matthew 25:31-46 is sometimes read as if it means, "Be good to those in need, and you will be all right on the day of judgment." This is a kind of humanistic gospel, in which we are saved by our own good deeds. However, such deeds are not sufficient for eternal salvation. Only Christ's work on the cross can accomplish that, and it can become yours only through faith. But nevertheless, we as Christians are absolutely called to do good to needy people all over the world.

Others have taken the passage to mean, "You must be good to your fellow Christians in need all over the world, Christians who are in prison and persecuted and so forth. Doing this will ensure that you will be all right on the day of judgment." And again, we do need to do good to our brothers and sisters all over the world who are persecuted because of their faith, as many are. Many of them are in great need. Indeed, every year, hundreds and thousands of martyrs give their lives in countries around the globe.

But what the Lord really meant when He pointed to those around Him was: "Whatever you did to one of the least of these brothers of Mine, you have done to Me." What did the nations do with the Jews in their midst? This is apparently a basis for judgment of the nations, with the separation of sheep-nations from goat-nations. What did the Church do with the Jews in her midst? What did we do with the Jews around us? For the Lord really means business. He does not very often speak about eternal hellfire, but in this passage He does: *"Depart from Me, you who are cursed, into the eternal fire prepared for the devil and his angels"* (Matt. 25:41b).

By and large, the Church has been silent as the Jews have been abused. Furthermore, the Church has often not only been a silent observer of horrors, but even an instigator through its blind theological thought systems. Israel may be blind, hardened in part with regard to the Gospel (painters and sculptors traditionally depict her as blindfolded), but the Church itself has been and is often even more blind, ignoring the clear teaching of the Bible regarding the Jewish people and Israel.

Even though many in the Church have no idea what is going on today with regard to the return of the Jews to the Promised Land, and where this all will lead to, still there is needed an admission of guilt and a commitment to repentance in unequivocal declarations to the Jewish people. But words alone are not enough; there must also be deeds of righteousness and compassion to provide proof of absolute and sincere apology and solidarity. We should bring forth true fruits worthy of repentance. We must imitate those Dutch Christians, such as Corrie ten Boom's family and many others, who gave their lives to defend the Jews when one of the antichrists of history, Hitler, appeared on the scene. They stood with the Jews against the enemies of the Jewish people and of God (see Ps. 83:5-6). Moreover, they not only supported Christian Jews but were there for all Jews. Those Dutch Christians knew that the Jews were the people of God, His chosen people, His firstborn!

We, too, can do our part. It is already a miracle that after 2000 years of Church history, Jews are willing to shake hands with us and accept some humanitarian aid! Thus, we can encourage Jews wherever possible and whenever they permit us to do so, helping them to return home to Israel from their worldwide exile and assist them in Israel.

We can support the Jews in Israel by giving humanitarian aid to those who have been psychologically and physically traumatized by war and terrorists attacks. We can also attempt to give moral and financial support to resist any form of economic boycott by the surrounding countries. We can stand with them politically, reminding them to "Trust in the Lord, trust in the Word. He is your God, the God of Israel. He will not leave you nor forsake you even if everyone else abandons you." We can tell them, like Isaiah

52:7b says: "[Don't despair.] *Your God reigns!*" We can be the first ones to protest about new flares of anti-Semitism; and we can make it clear that when Jews are threatened, we as Christians have to be taken on first by these demonic attacks. We as Christians should be like a protective shield. Actions like these will begin to reveal to Jews that perhaps something good can come from the followers of Jesus of Nazareth, and not just bloodshed. Then they will start to see that there is a difference between Christendom and true Christians.

Our actions can in a sense even help to prepare the way for His coming. Although we cannot hasten the day of His coming by whatever we do (because it is the decision of the Father when He will tell His Son to go back to earth), we can prepare the way, as Second Peter 3:11-13 points out. *"Prepare ye the way,"* John the Baptist preached (Matt. 3:3; Luke 3:4 KJV). Guilt must be acknowledged and deeply felt by us all. It is cheap to point our fingers at others, and say: "Those churches were responsible," or "The Europeans did this." We must identify with the guilt of the Church. We must become like Daniel.

IDENTIFYING WITH THE GUILTY

Personally, Daniel had done nothing wrong. But when he saw that the 70 years of the Babylonian captivity were almost over and that the return of the Jews to the Promised Land was imminent, he did not say: "Let's see how nicely prophecy will be fulfilled right before our very eyes." Instead, he went to his knees, and said, "Lord, forgive my sins." Then he said, *"We have sinned and done wrong"* (Dan. 9:5a; see also verses 3-19). He identified with the sins of his people, although he himself was a righteous man, who trusted in God in a hostile environment and remained true even to his Jewish dietary laws, in spite of the potential risks (see Dan. 1:8-15). It could have cost him his life, but he would rather have been right with God than save his own skin. Daniel did not point his finger at others. Rather, this pious man identified himself with the guilt of his people. *"We have sinned,"* he said. He even repented on behalf of his forefathers, the generations gone by.

Like him, every Christian, as part of the Christian Church in all ages and places, should say, "We have sinned." To do so will bring new life to the Church, a renewal of the faith, and perhaps even revival; but as long as there are unconfessed sins and guilt in the life of a person or a corporate body, the Holy Spirit cannot give His full blessing. This principle holds true for individuals as well as the entire Church. How can the Church meet with Jesus when He comes in glory, with Jewish blood upon her hands? The blood of ages? The way to life is not to be proud in our relationship with the Jewish people, but to be humble. We have to repent with words (as few as possible) and with deeds (as many as possible). Who knows what the Lord will still do for Israel and for the nations of the world when He sees His Church repent and change her ways? He might give us some more time, like He did with Jonah. We leave that up to Him.

PRAYER IS ALL IMPORTANT

Our task is to clear away the rubble of ages and to fill the breaches with prayer. We are to be watchmen on Zion's walls, continually seeking the Lord in prayer for mercy for His people.

We are to obey the biblical injunction to *"Pray for the peace of Jerusalem"* (Ps. 122:6a). To do so is to pray for an outpouring of the Holy Spirit on the inhabitants of Jerusalem and of the whole land. It is to pray for the nations round about Israel, to whom the Lord has also promised His blessings. It is to remind the Lord of the promises He has made and to humbly ask Him to fulfill them, just as some of the great saints in the Bible prayed. Praying for the peace of Jerusalem is ultimately praying for the Prince of Peace to come to Jerusalem, who will finally bring peace to the whole world. It is praying for the coming of the Kingdom, just as Jesus taught us in the Lord's Prayer. The Kingdom has always been the hope of the Church, her real Christian hope. The apostles said with all the longing of their hearts: "Maranatha! Come Lord Jesus!" And as long as He tarries, may the grace of the Lord Jesus Christ be with us all (see 1 Cor. 16:22-24; Rev. 22:20-21).

CONTACT THE AUTHOR

Rev. Willem J.J. Glashouwer
Christians for Israel International

P.O. Box 1100
3860 BC Nijkerk
Holland

Tel: 31 33 245 8824
Fax: 31 33 246 3644
Email: wglashouwer@c4israel.org

Additional copies of this book and other book titles from DESTINY IMAGE EUROPE are available at your local bookstore.

We are adding new titles every month!

To view our complete catalog online, visit us at:
www.eurodestinyimage.com

Send a request for a catalog to:

Via Acquacorrente, 6
65123 - Pescara - ITALY
Tel. +39 085 4716623 - Fax +39 085 9431270

"Changing the world, one book at a time."

Are you an author?

Do you have a "today" God-given message?

CONTACT US

We will be happy to review your manuscript for a possible publishing:

publisher@eurodestinyimage.com